CITY AND COUNTY MANAGEMENT 1929 — 1990

A RETROSPECTIVE

Institute of Public Administration

First published 1991
Institute of Public Administration
57-61 Lansdowne Road
Dublin, Ireland
Tel: (01) 697011 (Publications)
Fax: (01) 698644

ISBN 1-872002-51-X hardback
ISBN 1-872002-50-1 paperback

Cover and typographic design
by Butler Claffey Design
Origination by Keystrokes Limited
Printed by Criterion Press Limited
Dublin

MANAGE
1929 — 1990

A RETROSPECTIVE

Philip Monahan, (1894-1983). Cork City Manager, 1929-1958.

To the memory of Philip Monahan

CONTENTS

EDITORIAL GROUP
Joseph Boland (Chairman), former Clare County Manager

Richard Haslam, Head, Department of Public Administration, University College, Cork and former Limerick County Manager

Brian Johnston, Cavan County Manager

Brendan Kiernan, former Legal Adviser, Department of the Environment

James O'Donnell, Assistant Director General, Institute of Public Administration

Gerald Ward, Kildare County Manager

CONTRIBUTORS
Eunan O'Halpin, Senior Lecturer in Government and Public Administration, Dublin Business School, Dublin City University

Dr O'Halpin holds a BA and MA from University College, Dublin and a PhD from Cambridge University. He is the author of *Decline of the Union: British Government in Ireland 1892-1920* (1987) and *Head of the Civil Service: A Study of Sir Warren Fisher* (1989). He is preparing books on internal security since independence and on the administrative system.

Michael J. Bannon, Senior Lecturer, Department of Regional and Urban Planning, University College, Dublin

Dr Bannon holds a BA from University College, Dublin, an MA from the University of Alberta and a PhD from Dublin University. He has published widely on aspects of planning in Ireland and overseas. Forthcoming publications include reports on urbanisation and urban growth, producer services, and Ireland's international trade.

FOREWORD

It is just over sixty years since the management system was introduced to the Irish local government service. The County and City Managers' Association considered it an appropriate moment to commission a work on the origins of what has been one of the outstanding administrative innovations in the Irish system of government. *City and County Management 1929-1990: A Retrospective* goes beyond its initial modest objective and presents data of interest to the student of local government in general.

How to strike a balance between the responsibilities in the public service of democratic representatives and the administration is a perennial political question. In local government Ireland's response has been a unique one: a partnership between a democratically elected council and an official responsible for management, concerned alike with the physical, social, economic and cultural development of the the area of the local authority.

City and County Management 1929-1990: A Retrospective focuses on the role of managers in the local government system in Ireland since its introduction in Cork city in 1929. The introduction of the management system to local authorities marked a fundamental change in their operation. This volume describes the origins of the system and its contribution to local and national development. The career profiles of those who have held the offices of city and county managers give a glimpse of the men who have been attracted to the service. The chronology provides stepping-stones through the history of local government in the period, while the bibliography provides researchers and students with a practical guide to further study.

The management system has drawn attention from those outside the country to the local government system in Ireland. It has been the subject of study and research by academics, specialists and practitioners of local government services and by public representatives and review bodies on local government reform in such countries as England, Scotland, United States of America, Australia, New Zealand, Denmark, Holland and France. More recently, the Irish local government system and the role of the manager in this system have been studied by students from many countries in Africa that have secured independence from colonial rule. These students have attended training courses organised by the Institute of Public Administration. *City and County Management 1929-1990: A Retrospective* will help, then, in the area of comparative study.

Of the ninety-three men who hold or have held the offices of city and county manager since 1929, more than two-thirds have retired or are deceased. *City and County Management 1929-1990: A Retrospective* may also be seen as a commemoration of their work.

I would like to thank the Institute of Public Administration and its Director General for publishing *City and County Management 1929-1990: A Retrospective* at the request of the County and City Managers' Association. The work is a welcome addition to the many publications which the Institute has already published on local government topics in Ireland; and of course it is particularly appropriate that there should be a publication on the role of the city and county management system in Irish local government having regard to the interest shown in the system from outside the country.

I would like to thank Joseph Boland, former Clare County Manager, and chairman of the editorial group, for his inspiring dedication and commitment to the project. To the other members of the editorial group, who have assisted with information, research and documentation, thanks are also due.

I would like to thank those who gave assistance to the editorial group in their work and who helped in verifying dates and other historical information.

Finally, I would like to thank the special contributors to the book for their painstaking research and for the work they have undertaken in checking and verifying information — an endeavour necessary to ensure that the publication will be a valuable addition to the corpus on local government in Ireland as well as a worthy tribute to all those who have served their country by serving their county.

John Gerald Ward
Chairman
County and City Managers' Association

31 October 1990

PREFACE

We are indebted to many persons and to many organisations in the preparation of this volume. Dr T.J. Barrington, Professor Basil Chubb and Professor James Dooge gave us advice and encouragement at the beginning of the project. Dr Michael Bannon and Dr Eunan O'Halpin readily accepted a commission to contribute. We thank Maureen Conroy for compiling the bibliography.

We thank the local authorities, state bodies and the other organisations and persons who cooperated with us. We especially thank the Local Appointments Commission for their exceptional assistance, involving painstaking research in their own records and in the National Archives.

We thank the Institute of Public Administration for providing secretarial assistance and word-processing facilities. In particular we thank the Institute's Librarian Mary Prendergast and her staff. We are also grateful to the Institute for permission to reproduce the profile of Philip Monahan which appeared in *Administration* Volume 2, 1954-55.

We are grateful to Mary O'Brien (daughter of Philip Monahan), the *Cork Examiner* and the County and City Managers' Association for supplying the photographs reproduced in the book.

I wish to thank my colleagues on the Editorial Group for their commitment and advice. It would be remiss of me if I did not thank in particular James O'Donnell for devoting so much of his time to this project and for his unfailing patience.

For me this has been a labour of love. It has sharpened memories of friends deceased, friends retired and friends still serving.

Many absences from home have been necessary. For her understanding, I thank Catherine, my wife.

Joseph Boland
Chairman, Editorial Group

31 October 1990

I
THE ORIGINS
OF CITY AND COUNTY
MANAGEMENT

Eunan O'Halpin

Local government in the twentieth century

The development of the local authority management system, like most innovations in Irish government, was somewhat haphazard. What are now regarded as its key attributes are not quite the ones originally intended for it. From the Cork City Management Act of 1929 to the eventual establishment of a national local authority management system in 1942, it is clear that central government saw the appointment of managers with statutory powers independent of local politicians partly as a means of exerting greater national or central control over local affairs. The history of the system since its inception suggests that managers have formed a very different view of their functions and their standing in relation both to local authorities and to central government.[1]

There were considerable reforms in local government during the early years of independence. These arose partly from a pressing need to re-establish order after the civil war, and partly from a set of general assumptions about how to provide for the efficient, economical and honest organisation of public business. But the reforms also owed a lot to the actual operation of the 1898 Local Government Act. This law partly democratised local government in Ireland, without, however, cleaning it up. Under the act local administrative power was concentrated in the hands of councils responsible to a restricted ratepaying electorate. Day to day control over the detailed administration of local affairs lay in the hands of committees of part-time councillors. Outside Ulster the majority of these were associated with the main nationalist group, the Nationalist Party.

Irish local government in the first decades of the twentieth century acquired a reputation for amateurishness, incompetence, venality and political favouritism, Dublin Corporation being the most notorious example.[2] The extent to which all local authorities could fairly be tarred with the same brush is an open question, although there is no doubt that appointments to official posts were the subject of much intrigue everywhere. It suited the purposes both of advanced separatist groups like Sinn Féin and of committed unionists to denigrate the conduct of local affairs by the Nationalist Party, which until 1918 appeared set fair to become the party of government under home rule. Propertied interests, particularly commercial and agricultural ratepayers, were routinely critical of local administration on grounds of extravagance and waste — categories of profligacy which appeared to embrace most

2

social spending. Social reformers, never a particularly significant group in Irish public life, argued that local government did far too little. While municipal administration in particular was subject to constant criticism, however, there was no consensus either on its precise defects or on a better alternative.

Although some consideration was given to further changes in local government structures in the years following the 1898 act, this was largely incidental to efforts to devise an acceptable constitutional alternative to home rule which would grant the substance of self-government for all of Ireland without endangering the union with Great Britain. Sir Antony MacDonnell's ill-fated Irish Council bill of 1907, in the words of its author 'essentially a development of the existing system of Local Government in Ireland', envisaged an elaborate legislative and administrative structure, subordinate to the British parliament, in which the under secretary for Ireland — the most senior civil servant — would sit with and be on a par with elected politicians as this 'will tend to prevent friction and to promote the efficient despatch of public business'.[3] However, it was only the passing of the Home Rule Act in 1914, and the struggle for complete independence from 1916 to 1921, which changed the climate for Irish administration. Irish politicians of all persuasions showed themselves anxious to depart from the system of government in Ireland operated by the British, advocating sundry changes all of which were in some degree centralist in spirit. From the record of secret discussions held in Dublin in 1915, it is clear that the leaders of the Nationalist Party envisaged a highly centralised system of government under home rule, including a 'Ministry of Local Affairs and Public Health', in contrast to the diffuse structures through which Britain attempted to govern Ireland. They believed, too, that public spending would have to be sharply reduced. Greater efficiency would ensure some savings, but they also assumed that British standards of social provision could not be maintained because the country could not afford them.[4] The Irish Convention of 1917-18, where constitutional Irish political groups met to find an agreed settlement of the self-government issue, made broadly similar assumptions about economical administration and about increased central government control of public life. It agreed on the abolition of unpaid magistrates, the backbone of the Irish legal system at local level which was closely tied to local government structures. (To the consternation of the British authorities

3

the chairman of Kerry County Council became a justice of the peace *ex officio* in 1918 while in jail for possession of explosives.) The convention also rejected the concept of local police forces on the British mainland model. It accepted the need to standardise and professionalise public service appointments through a strong Civil Service Commission, though with safeguards to protect the interests of Protestant Ulster, and generally adopted a reformist perspective on administrative questions. (It is worth noting that to the end of British rule in Ireland an abnormally high number of appointments at every level in central bureaucracy were made by nomination rather than by competitive examination, in contrast to the meritocratic system developed in Britain itself in the course of the nineteenth century, and that promotions were heavily influenced by political and religious considerations. The consequent problems of widespread patronage and of inefficiency were not confined to local government).[5]

Sinn Féin was, therefore, going with the tide of political opinion in its hostility to the prevailing structure and practices of local administration, in its social conservatism, and in its equation of reform with economy, standardisation and increased direction from central government. This was scarcely a dynamic vision. The movement had considerable success in conscripting local authorities in support of the independence struggle from 1918 to 1921, frequently bringing them into conflict with the Local Government Board and with the law on issues such as rating and criminal injuries. From 1919 this activity was co-ordinated by the Dáil local government department under W.T. Cosgrave and Kevin O'Higgins, later to become key figures in the first Free State governments. In July 1921, Cosgrave reported approvingly that 'the destruction of the Custom House has finally eliminated the British Local Government Board as a serious factor in the situation.' The disappearance of one central authority was, however, not to presage greater freedom for local government. Cosgrave 'thought it wise to increase the number of Inspectors from 14 to 20', while the 'urgent' question of the 'extension' of 'the audit of the accounts of public bodies' was 'a natural and necessary development' which, rather implausibly, he claimed some local authorities were 'eager' to see.[6] As well as giving them an early taste for central control of local government, Cosgrave and O'Higgins learnt an obvious lesson from the use of local councils to subvert British rule: the more leeway such bodies had, the

4

more these could embarrass and defy central government. After independence they took steps to thwart republicans attempting to use the same tactics against them.

The Cosgrave governments of 1922-32 were impatient at the defects of the administrative system they inherited from the British. They quickly reshaped central government through the establishment of the impartial Civil Service Commission in 1923 to control appointments, and through the rationalisation of departments under the Ministers and Secretaries Act of 1924, when the Department of Local Government and Public Health (referred to hereafter as 'the department') was renamed.[7] In local administration the challenge was, if anything, greater. Many areas had suffered severely during the war of independence and the subsequent civil war, and after years of disruption local authorities were ill-prepared financially and administratively to carry out the necessary repairs and reconstruction. Some councils and boards were dominated by republicans who declined to carry out statutory functions such as striking a rate. In other cases sheer administrative incompetence and inertia meant that urgent problems went unaddressed. In addition to the administrative and political residue of the civil war, the structure of Irish local government was patently in need of revision to take account of changed conditions and requirements in both urban and rural areas.

Once the civil war was over the government acted vigorously to impose its will on local authorities and to rationalise local administrative structures. The 1923 Local Government (Temporary Provisions) Act gave the Minister for Local Government (referred to hereafter as 'the minister') power to suspend local authorities which, through incompetence or design, were not discharging their proper functions, and to replace them for a limited period with a government-appointed commissioner. Ernest Blythe, who was the minister throughout the civil war, later gave a somewhat apologetic defence of this measure in a letter to a constituent written in November 1924. He attacked the dilatory attitude of the Monaghan and Carrickmacross rural district councils, which had met only four and six times respectively in the past year, though even this was a somewhat better performance than was put up by councils 'in many other parts of the country'. He continued:

I am as much opposed as anyone could be to having the work of local Councils carried out by officials appointed by the Central Government. I am absolutely in favour of local control. I believe that the Central Government acquires quite enough unpopularity in administering its own Departments without adding to the burden by undertaking responsibility for administration which ought to be purely local.[8]

However, the difficulty persisted that many local authorities appeared incapable of behaving responsibly, and the minister's power of dissolution was made permanent in the 1925 Local Government Act, a law which included a number of significant measures. Rural district councils were abolished and a standard superannuation system for all local authority employees was introduced. In the same year, legislation on combined purchasing was passed, and in 1926 the Local Appointments Commission, 'something of a wonder in Irish political culture', was established to oversee the impartial selection of senior local authority officials.[9] Through such measures central government laid down uniform standards and procedures for local government nationally, and took powers to compel local authorities to observe them. They contributed to the professionalisation of local authority service, and to the diminution of political and personal influence in administrative matters. They consequently reduced the administrative and discretionary power of local councillors, which was precisely what was intended.

These innovations reflected a desire for greater efficiency in local administration and a disdain for the traditional workings of local politics. They also had a wider political dimension. The Cosgrave government was hostile to the way the local government system worked not only on account of inefficiency and corruption but also because it afforded their republican opponents both a useful platform and a means of embarrassing the government. In June 1925 an American diplomat in Dublin reported the views of the minister, Seamus de Burca. De Burca told him that the 1898 act had been used for national political purposes by Sinn Féin during the independence struggle. After the Treaty,

the Republicans continued to utilize the local bodies as forms for the expression of their dissent and as a means of embarrassing the conduct of Government. That is to say, they continued to use

6

against the Free State Government exactly the same tactics as the old Irish movement had used against the British Government ... The Minister ... said to me that while he could not hope that partisanship would be eliminated from the local government bodies altogether, he did have hopes that a distinct advance in that direction would be obtained.[10]

Although from 1926 the new Fianna Fáil party attempted to make some political capital out of the government's treatment of local authorities, what evidence there is suggests that the general public was, at worst, indifferent to the reforms introduced. The Cosgrave government was, accordingly, usually unmoved by the protests which its actions provoked from the local politicians and notables whose influence, especially in the sensitive matter of local authority jobs, they undermined. In 1927 Richard Mulcahy, then the minister, bluntly informed an importunate reverend mother that he would not intercede in an appointment because 'everything ... possible has been done to do away with patronage or favouritism throughout the whole of our Public Service — Governmental or Local.'[11] With the arguable exception of the Dunbar-Harrison case in 1930, all governments appear to have viewed the decisions of the Local Appointments Commission as sacrosanct ever since, an extraordinary legacy for which even its most bitter critics have praised the Cosgrave government.[12]

The idea of city management

The thrust of the Cosgrave government's local government policy was to impose uniform standards and to increase central control. Although the key issue of appointments was addressed through the establishment of the Local Appointments Commission, the government took no other initiative permanently to adjust the relationship between bureaucrats and politicians at local level. Although it occurred in a climate of positive reform, therefore, development of the concept of local authority management was haphazard.

Beginning with Kerry County Council in 1923, the government had taken to dissolving troublesome or ineffective local authorites and imposing commissioners to run their affairs for a limited period. Most of the first generation of commissioners were civil servants of the department. Although conceived as a temporary punitive measure

7

intended to force local politicians to behave more responsibly when they resumed office, the substitution of bureaucrats for elected councillors generally had what the department termed 'salutory effects' on administration in the authorities concerned.[13] From the government's point of view commissioners had two outstanding characteristics: political reliability and administrative competence. The department certainly found them more respectful of the law, and probably more amenable to central direction, than the councils they replaced. So far from engendering hostility in the local electorate, furthermore, commissioners became the objects of local praise for their efficiency and frugality.[14] This suggested two things: that local affairs were better administered under the day-to-day control of a full-time official than by an assortment of part-time councillors, and that the public — or at least that minority of the public who had the right to vote in local elections — were more interested in the cost and adequacy of local services than in the question of who controlled them. The dissolution of the corporations of both Dublin and Cork in 1924, in each case after somewhat perfunctory inquiries into their affairs, created an opportunity for a thorough examination of the state of municipal government, something for which influential groups of ratepayers in both cities had been pressing for some time. For Dublin the minister initially hoped to make do with a 'departmental Committee of Inquiry', thought likely to be more effective and less susceptible to political pressures.[15] In the event, however, circumstances dictated that he establish a Greater Dublin Commission, where his misgivings were borne out. Its remit was broad, to:

> examine the several laws and the practice affecting the adminis-tration of local and public utility services, including local represent-ation and taxation throughout the Capital City of Dublin, and the County of Dublin and to recommend such changes as may be desirable.[16]

The commission took evidence on every aspect of local administration, including systems of municipal government abroad, and reported after two years. The proceedings were, unfortunately, monopolised by the chairman, a professor of metaphysics apparently possessed of all the weaknesses of his calling, who so bored the other members that they left him to draw up its conclusions.[17] These were heavily influenced by a ratepayers' lobby, the Greater Dublin Movement, and reflected a prevailing contempt in educated circles for elective local democracy. The commission's report called for a 'Unitary Government' within 'Greater Dublin', an area in which 'there now function some nineteen thinking and spending authorities'. The twin aims of 'democratic control' and 'efficient management' would be met by establishing a 'scheme of City Management under an elective Council', which 'accords with the best experience of the United States, Germany and the more progressive Cantons of Switzerland'. There would be a 'Chief Executive Officer who would be styled and known as a City Manager', assisted by an 'Advisory Board' consisting of the heads of the various departments within the corporation. He would be responsible to an emasculated council for the administration of the new county borough. Most of the elective offices of the existing local authorities would disappear, along with those of the Lord Mayor, 'his Swordbearer, his Macebearer, and his Marshal' which 'have little else to recommend them than their ancient standing'. The Mansion House would then 'be released for public purposes', perhaps including an art gallery, museum and a lending library, and 'would provide, too, a Municipal Concert Hall, wherein the Feis Ceoil might find that accommodation for which it has been too long kept waiting', a proposal which neatly combined civic utility, imported concepts of modern municipal administration, and due deference to the nation's Gaelic heritage.[18]

The government baulked at these proposals, and reverted to the minister's original idea of remitting the Dublin problem to a departmental committee.[19] But the Greater Dublin Commission's report was of some significance as the first quasi-official endorsement of the suggestion that a distinction in law should be made between the functions of elected politicians and of permanent officials in local government. That idea had been in circulation in Ireland for some time — in 1924 a Donegal county councillor called for the appointment of a 'managing director' to run his county's affairs — thanks largely to the efforts of a Cork solicitor, John J. Horgan. Drawing inspiration from innovations in American municipal government since the turn of the century, he had argued the case for something similar in Ireland, where prevailing methods of city administration, he commented in 1923, 'would disgrace a native village in Central Africa'.[20] Although county management was not yet in sight, for city government it was the respective powers and responsibilities of elected municipal representatives and chief executives,

rather than the principle of separating politics and administration, that remained to be worked out.

Despite Horgan's energetic advocacy, it was apparently a matter of administrative expediency which determined that Cork city was the first to acquire a manager. Indeed, early in 1927, the department thought the city would not be the subject of a 'special Bill', as the minister was contemplating legislation 'to alter the form of management of all County Boroughs other than the City of Dublin'.[21] In its unusually frank annual report for 1928-29 the department stated that the performance of the Dublin and Cork commissioners had shown 'the managerial system' to be 'especially suitable'. Because 'the problem in the metropolis was complicated by intricate questions of area, finance, and town planning', however, Cork was the first to receive legislative attention. The problem there was to 'effect a centralisation of executive responsibility in one managerial head under a system analogous to that which had been attended by such good results during the commissioner's term of office', while providing for an elected council to set policy. Following a visit in January 1928 by the minister to Cork to confer with 'local representatives', a bill was approved by the government in June 1928 and brought before the Dáil.[22]

General Mulcahy commended the 'rather simple and uncomplicated measure' to the Dáil. It provided for the establishment of the office of city manager, to be filled by the incumbent commissioner Philip Monahan, and for the statutory division of 'executive' and 'reserved' functions between the manager and the new fifteen-man city council.[23] Although it did not encounter concerted opposition, its passage took longer than expected, and it was the subject of quite lively discussion. Opinions varied amongst both government and opposition TDs about it, although few speakers argued for a straightforward return to the old system of election by wards and administration by committee. After four years of distinctly autocratic rule by Monahan, who despite his own stint in local politics in Drogheda had no time at all for elected councillors and did not attempt to conceal this from them, Cork deputies were divided on the merits of having a permanent manager. A Labour TD complained that the bill was the brainchild of 'the most reactionary class in Cork city' who 'could never, under any circumstances, get elected to a public body themselves,' and who had brought about the dissolution of Cork corporation in 1924. A party colleague described Monahan as

10

384881

'no friend of the working classes'. The Fianna Fáil TD Martin Corry, a Cork county councillor and an inveterate critic of Cork city, warned of 'the hidden hand, to set up the puppet acting as a cloak for the dictatorship of the Executive Council'. He called Monahan 'this political partisan'. Another Fianna Fáil TD, Seán French, who had been lord mayor at the time of Cork corporation's dissolution, supported the principle of the bill but complained that 'I want a City Manager appointed and not a city master.' On the other hand, a government TD said he had been 'deluged with representations ... the consensus of opinion in the city of Cork' was that the bill 'is a courageous, honest and able attempt ... to grapple with a very difficult situation.'[24]

Dublin Fianna Fáil TDs rightly saw the bill as the precursor of further legislation covering their own city. Seán Lemass said there should be more councillors. He agreed that the old system of election by ward was unsatisfactory but doubted whether 'ward patriotism' could be eliminated. Gerry Boland opposed it in its entirety: 'I stand for autocracy at headquarters in national affairs and for a bigger extension of freedom in local affairs.' That would be 'far more desirable than having the centralised control of local affairs in Dublin'. (Ironically his son Kevin was the minister who dissolved Dublin Corporation for refusing to strike a rate forty-one years later.) Eamon de Valera, who had no direct experience of local government, nevertheless made an interesting contribution. He saw that the bill contained 'principles ... which are likely to be extended' elsewhere. He deplored 'the grudging way it is proposed to give back to the people of Cork the right of governing themselves locally', but welcomed 'the fact that we are at last giving up this idea of keeping all power centralised in Dublin'. He supported 'the general idea of separating the deliberative functions from the executive powers ... an idea that I, personally, thought might be applied to a much wider sphere than merely to ... city government'.[25] In the course of its passage the bill was amended to increase the number of councillors from fifteen to twenty one, but otherwise went through unscathed and became law in February 1929. The Cork bill was eulogized by John J. Horgan in an American journal, the *National Municipal Review*. His article was, ironically in view of his faith in city government in Ohio, immediately followed by a piece headed 'Election frauds and councilmanic scandals stir Cleveland', describing how 'revelations of graft with subsequent indictments and convictions of city

11

officials ... have renewed activity in favour of abolishing the city manager charter.'[26] No such fate befell Philip Monahan.

Monahan, born in Dublin in 1894, had been a schoolteacher and Sinn Féin activist in Drogheda. In 1920 he was elected to Drogheda Corporation and to Louth County Council on an anti-corruption ticket, and became mayor of Drogheda the same year. He was, apparently, lured to Kerry as its first commissioner in 1923 by the offer of a handsome salary, a car and a gun. A year later he moved on to Cork when its corporation was dissolved. This is not the place for detailed discussion of his work as commissioner and manager. Although a very efficient administrator, what mattered most were the high standards of integrity and of independence which he set from local politics and, equally important for the management system, from central government. Whatever else could be said of his thirty-four years in Cork, he was never the minister's or the mayor's man.[27]

In December 1929, the government agreed to introduce a bill to deal with the complicated situation in Dublin. In addition to the incorporation of long-standing local authority areas into the new county borough, the department proposed the installation of a manager, saying that it:

> is not aware that any difficulty has yet become apparent in the managerial machine provided in Cork, the relations between the Council and the Manager on the whole appear to be harmonious. It was contended during the Dáil Debates on the Bill that the Manager would be too closely associated with the Minister to be regarded as a sufficiently independent factor in local affairs. So far as the Cork City Manager is concerned the Department's experience is that since the executive side of local administration was vested in him he has shown an independence of thought and initiative that did not require the intervention of the Department in phases of local administration that had [hitherto] often required a great deal of careful supervision on the part of the Central Department.

The bill was not well received in the Oireachtas, both because of the extensive powers it gave to the manager, and because it granted the franchise to ratepaying business as well as to individuals. With the exception of the Labour Party, which consistently opposed both city and county management in the Oireachtas, most TDs accepted the principle of giving executive responsibilities to a manager, while querying the extent of his powers. What eventually emerged was, in the words of a Fianna Fáil critic, 'a very different Bill' from that introduced, 'and a better measure in some respects'. While unhappy about the discretionary powers of the manager, the Dublin deputy Seán T. O'Kelly welcomed the appointment of the Dublin town clerk, Gerald Sherlock, 'a good official, and they had to pass over all their own pets', the three commissioners who had run the municipality since the council's dissolution in 1924. The bill became law in July 1930.[28] The impact on city administration was less dramatic than in Cork. Whether this was a function of the complexity of Dublin's affairs, or because Sherlock, as some maintain, in contrast to his abrasive counterpart in Cork city, remained town clerk in all but name, is still a matter of opinion. It cannot be settled until more research has been done.

In 1934, Limerick corporation sought and obtained a city management act, while in 1939 a similar measure was passed for the remaining county borough, Waterford, where the city council had been dissolved in May 1937.[29] In Waterford there was no great demand for a manager, but Roche suggests that the government felt obliged to deal with it as the last unreformed county borough before introducing a national county management measure.[30]

County Management

The eventual introduction of county management under the 1940 County Management Act was preceded by a decade of uncertainty about the reorganisation of rural administration. There was some pressure for change: the Poor Law Commission of 1925-27 recommended that local health administration should be taken over by the county councils, 'acting through paid officials'.[31] Writing in the *Irish Local Government Annual, 1930-31*, however, John Garvin of the department seemed to suggest no great changes were on the way. He contrasted the technical and administrative complexity of municipal affairs with the relatively more straightforward tasks of rural councils, observing that developments in:

13

urban organisation ... must needs emphasise a sharp dividing line between urban and rural services. The great majority of rural ratepayers, while their districts remain strictly rural, will admittedly be content with the minimum of social service, together with the minimum of rating burden afforded under county organisation.[32]

Nevertheless, despite the absence of a reform lobby the success of city management gave food for thought to those concerned with county administration. In May 1931, the Minister for Finance stated that the county councils would be reduced in membership and managers appointed along the same lines as in Cork and Dublin. His government lost office before taking any action on this, but nine years later Cosgrave told the Dáil they had intended to introduce such changes.[33] The Fianna Fáil administration which came into office in 1932 was outwardly better disposed towards the traditional structures; in practice, however, any sympathy ministers may have had soon evaporated. In the autumn of 1933 the government agreed that the minister should submit proposals 'to provide for the adoption of a [county] managerial system' and the postponement of local elections, and he told the Dáil that he intended to establish an enquiry to see whether the principles of city management might be applied to county administration.[34] Nothing more was heard of this in public for some years, but the department put forward radical proposals to the government in March 1934. In a remarkably intemperate explanatory memorandum it argued for the gradual merging of national and local administration, and the phasing out of locally elected councils. As an interim measure, managers would be appointed and given powers hitherto exercised by councillors. While new councils would be elected, their 'retention ... is intended as a transitory measure', and their 'func-tions ... shall be wholly advisory and they shall have no administrative or executive functions'. Managers would ultimately become 'State officials', all local councils would disappear, and national and local taxation would be merged. The 'necessity for reform' was overwhelming: the 'existing system ... is defective and unsatisfactory'. Local councils 'are a relic of British administration when the people sought for the control of popular bodies' for national political reasons. With the:

establishment of a Central Administration responsible to the people as a whole and with modern improvements in transport and

14

communications, governmental intervention and supervision is now feasible in respect of all national activities. The retention of local government bodies is, therefore, gradually becoming an expensive anachronism.

Furthermore, the 'actual conduct of local administration is also unsatisfactory', due to 'the intrusion of worthless and irrelevant political discussions in respect of which the local body has no direct functions and which often retard and prejudice the transaction of local business', to 'financial maladministration', to 'failure to fulfil duties and to comply with the law' and other sins.[35]

This was centralism writ large: even the managers were to come from the department's inspectorate until permanent arrangements could be made. In the event, the memorandum was withdrawn, and nothing more was heard of it. It is not surprising that the government should contemplate administrative reorganisation for local authorities, but the scope of the proposals put forward by the department, and the vehemence with which the entire framework of local government was condemned, was extraordinary, particularly given Fianna Fáil's political style at local level — as the Fine Gael TD James Dillon put it in 1939, if the government 'four years ago' had announced the introduction of a 'Managerial Bill ... the whole Fianna Fáil party would have fainted away in sickened horror'.[36] This is perhaps why, having prepared and then withdrawn this broadside, the department put forward nothing at all in its stead. The wild design for the complete elimination of local authorities was never heard of again. Even county management took some years to get back onto the government's agenda.

Although it shied away from reform of county administration, de Valera's government reacted to political challenges from local authorities just as sharply as its precedessor had done. In the summer of 1934, at the height of the struggle between the government and the Blueshirt movement, four county councils with anti-Fianna Fáil majorities refused to collect rates. They were promptly dissolved and commissioners appointed in their place.[37] In the following years, a number of other local authorities suffered the same fate, though on grounds of inefficiency rather than of politics. These continuing difficulties with local administration probably contributed to a gradual acceptance at cabinet level that thoroughgoing reform was both possible and desirable.

15

Confusion surrounds the eventual decision to introduce county management. Desmond Roche records John Collins's recollection of 'the surprise of the officials (himself included)' when Seán T. O'Kelly, the minister, informed the department that the government had agreed to the drafting of a bill 'without the hallowed preliminaries of neo-styled memoranda'.[38] The available records indicate that the proposal surfaced in May 1938, when Brian O'Nolan, the private secretary to the minister, forwarded 'a preliminary outline of proposals' for a 'County Management Bill', including the suggestion that 'the existing county secretaries might be made the first managers', to the Department of the Taoiseach. Some months later came a request that the cabinet consider whether a bill should be drafted. For some reason — perhaps the fate of the 1934 proposals, perhaps because the minister wanted to keep his department in the dark until the die was cast — O'Nolan would not submit a detailed memorandum despite pressure from the Department of the Taoiseach. The government gave general authority for a bill on the basis of a brief and sketchy outline of the main proposals. The bill ran into drafting difficulties, evidence perhaps that the department had been caught on the hop by the government decision. The main problems concerned the appointment and allocation of the first managers (some counties were to be paired for management purposes) and these delayed its progress.[39]

Although war had broken out by the time the bill eventually reached the Dáil in December 1939, no one adduced the expansion of administrative effort in areas such as rationing and civil defence in support of its provisions. It was received with evident distaste by some government deputies, notably Martin Corry of Cork, who once more attacked Philip Monahan, but they supported the minister when it came to voting. Their discomfiture made some Fine Gael TDs, who were allowed a free vote, all the more enthusiastic about it: James Dillon said anything would be better than the prevailing chaos, taunted Fianna Fáil as a party of local fixers, and blamed them for having turned 'local elections into political elections'. It was strongly opposed by the Labour Party: William Norton, the leader, read out extracts from the speeches of de Valera, O'Kelly and the minister P.J. Ruttledge opposing the Cork and Dublin bills, while a colleague spoke of reversion 'to a system worse even than the grand jury system'. Another claimed that 'the position ... will be that the county manager will be the 'yes-man' of the

Department', and that the Irish people 'now can well complain of the Hitlerism that is about to start in the Twenty Six Counties'.[40] But the bill went through without difficulty. It became law in June 1940, although it was not brought into operation until supporting legislation was enacted two years later.[41]

Conclusion

The precise form that city and county management was given in legislation from 1929 to 1940 owed a good deal to local exigency and to chance, and something to party politics. Irritation at the political posturing and obstructionism of some local authorities, as well as disquiet at their apparent inefficiency, undoubtedly strengthened the Cosgrave government's will to bring them to heel. The establishment of orderly municipal administration was a subset of the government's broader strategy of restoring the country to normality after years of political upheaval and violence. It was also part and parcel of an approach to domestic government common to the Nationalist Party, Sinn Féin, Cumann na nGaedhael and Fianna Fáil, in which local as distinct from national democracy was frowned on: an Irish administration, responsible to the Irish people and knowing their every wish, would not tolerate either inefficiency or insubordination from local authorities. While Cumann na nGaedhael's dislike of the intrusion of politics into local administration may have been stronger than Fianna Fáil's, de Valera's government proved just as intolerant a central authority of what it saw as local inefficiency, and just as willing to dilute the powers of local politicians.

City managers were not conceived of primarily as agents of central government. Rather, they were seen as skilled technicians, applying the antiseptic standards of scientific administration to matters previously dealt with in the unsavoury gutter of local politics. There is no doubt that the department had faith in their professionalism and their probity. Equally there is no evidence that it found them at all pliable where the interests of the locality were involved — indeed, it was harder to intervene in the affairs of a well run local authority than in one where public business was not being properly transacted. The adoption of the management principle in county government followed from the perceived success of the city schemes.

17

Notes

1. The management system is dealt with extensively in Desmond Roche, *Local government in Ireland* (Dublin, 1982) and Neil Collins, *Local government managers at work: the city and county manager system of local government in the Republic of Ireland* (Dublin, 1987).

   At the time of writing the records of the Department of the Environment were in the process of being transferred to the National Archives, under the provisions of the National Archives Act, and were not yet available for consultation. They will doubtless provide additional insights into the development and operation of the management system amongst many other aspects of local administration.

2. CS Andrews, *Dublin made me* (Dublin, 1979), pp31-2; JJ Lee, *Ireland 1912-1985: politics and society* (London, 1989), p.161.

3. On this see John Kendle, *Ireland and the federal solution: the debate over the United Kingdom constitution 1870-1921* (Montreal, 1989); MacDonnell to Bryce [chief secretary for Ireland], 3 Feb. 1906, MacDonnell papers, Bodleian library, MS Eng Hist c351. On the Irish Council bill and on MacDonnell's tempestuous tenure as under secretary from 1902 to 1908 see Eunan O'Halpin, *The decline of the union: British government in Ireland, 1892-1920* (Dublin, 1987), pp32-80. MacDonnell, 'the Tiger of Bengal', made his name as a civil servant in India, where officials in practice enjoyed pro-consular powers.

4. Minutes of 'informal conference on Irish Orders in Council', 17 Feb. and 10 Sept. 1915, Trinity College, Dublin, John Dillon MS 6801/161 and 186/A. By the latter date 'Public Health' had disappeared from the title though not the functions of the proposed ministry.

5. 'Report of the proceedings of the Irish Convention', *Parliamentary Papers* (1918) x, 712 and 815; Eunan O'Halpin, 'Ireland, 1854-1939', in Sabino Cassese and Jill Pellew (eds.), *Le systeme du merite: cahier d'histoire de l'administration no. 2* (Brussels, 1987), pp111-17, and *The decline of the union*, p.144.

6. Report to Dáil Éireann on 'Local Government Department', undated, July 1921, Trinity College, Dublin, Barton MS 7833/55; Roche, *Local government*, p.50.

7. In the 'Report of committee on the allocation of functions among government departments' [the Blythe committee] of 1923, on which the 1924 act was based, the department was provisionally called the 'Ministry of Health and Local Government'. N[ational] A[rchives, Dublin], Department of the Taoiseach papers, S1932.

8. Blythe to Thomas Toal, 25 Nov. 1924, UCD Archives, Blythe papers, p24/507.

9. Roche, *Local government*, pp52-4; Lee, *Ireland 1912-1985*, p.162. It should be noted that there were legislative precedents for the 1923 and 1925 acts at least as far back as the 1838 Poor Relief (Ireland) Act, which gave central government powers to suspend certain local authorities and appoint commissioners in their place. John Garvin, 'Nature and extent of central control over local government administration', in FC King (ed.), *Public administration in Ireland* vol. ii (Dublin, 1949), p.162.

10. CM Hathaway, Consul General, to State Department, 16 June 1925, United States National Archives, State Department, 841d00/776.

11. Mulcahy to 'My Dear Reverend Mother', 1 Dec. 1927, UCD Archives, Mulchay papers, P76/68.

12. Lee, *Ireland 1912-1985*, pp161-3; interview with Dr CS Andrews, 8 June 1982; Andrews, *Man of no property*, p.120. Dr Andrews made a sharp distinction between permanent appointments in central and local bureaucracy and those which remained in the government's gift.

13. Department of Local Government and Public Health, *Fourth Report 1928-29* (Dublin, 1930), p.16.

14. Ibid; *Report 1929-30* (Dublin, 1931), pp. 13-14; Roche, *Local government,* p.53.

15. Memorandum by EP McCarron, 25 Jan. 1924, NA S6532.

16. *Report of the Greater Dublin Commission of Inquiry* (Dublin, 1926), p.1 (copy in S6532 as in note 15 above).

17. Collins, *Local government managers,* p.24.

18. *Report of the Greater Dublin Commission of Inquiry,* pp2-3, 6.

19. As in note 15 above.

20. Quoted in Collins, *Local government managers,* p.25; information supplied by Donegal County Council. In *The Cork City Manager Act* (Cork, 1929), Horgan reiterates his claim to be the father of the concept. I am grateful to Richard Haslam for providing a copy of this work, and for his help generally in my research for this chapter.

21. Note by WJ Gilligan, private secretary to the minister, 1 Feb. 1927, NA, S5265.

22. *Fourth Report,* pp16-18, as note 13 above; the government's decision was taken on 7 June 1928, as noted in S5265; notes on the government's legislative agenda, 4 Oct. 1928 and 14 Feb. 1929, Mulcahy papers P7/C/86(2).

23. According to Roche, *Local government,* p.103, the legal distinction between reserved and executive functions derived from the home rule bills rather than from the Bombay Corporation Act of 1889 as is sometimes maintained.

24. *Dáil Debates* xxiv. cols. 1851-87, 28 June and xxv, cols. 371-406, 12 July 1928. This was the second stage discussion of the bill.

25. Ibid, 28 June 1928.

26. JJ Horgan, 'The Cork City Manager plan — an Irish experiment', *National Municipal Review* xvii, no.5(May 1929), pp.287-9, in NA, S5265. President Cosgrave thanked Horgan for the article, adding that 'what surprised me most was the news that you were the author of the new scheme.'

27. 'Silhouette', 'Philip Monahan', *Administration* 2(1), (1954), pp65-74; information from Mr. Richard Haslam.

28. Memorandum for the Executive Council, 15 Jan. 1930, NA, S6533; *Dáil Debates* xxxiv, cols. 2420-6, 22 May 1930. The substantive preceding stages are in *Dáil Debates* xxxiii, cols. 924-1016 and 1025-11170, and xxiv 707-804, 812-901, and 994-1048.

29. Papers on these bills are in NA, S6461 and S10533.

30. Roche, *Local government in Ireland,* p.104.

31. John Collins, *Local government* (2nd ed., prepared by Desmond Roche, Dublin, 1963), p.53.

32. John Garvin, 'The development of city government', *Irish Local Government Annual, 1930-31* (Dublin 1931), p.33 *Dail Debates* LXXVIII col. 1222, 7 Dec. 1939.

33. Roche, *Local government in Ireland,* p.105.

34. Desmond Roche, 'A memoir of the author', in Collins, *Local government,* p.8.

35. Memorandum by the Department of Local Government and Public Health, 1 Mar. 1934, NA, S6466.

36. Ibid; Roche, *Local government in Ireland,* p.105; *Dáil Debates* LXXVIII, col. 1009-10, 7 Dec. 1939.

37. Maurice Manning, *The Blueshirts* (Dublin, 1970), p.130.

38. Roche, 'A memoir of the author', p.33.

39. The papers are in NA, S10685 and S10685B.

40. *Dáil Debates* lxxviii, cols. 901-72, 5 Dec., and cols. 1182-1301, 7 Dec. 1939 contain the discussions on the second reading. It is ironic that the last deputy quoted above denouncing the excesses of centralisation and 'Hitlerism', James Everett, was to be the cause of the Baltinglass *cause célèbre* a decade later, when as Minister for Post and Telegraphs he intervened personally in a post office appointment on what were seen as party political grounds.

41. Roche, *Local government in Ireland*, pp105-7; papers on the 1942 legislation are in NA, S12729. The new system was the subject of a quite detailed but dull report from the American legation in Dublin to the State Department on 15 Mar. 1943, State Departments Records, 841D.00/1380.

   In the course of this research I consulted the papers of Mr. Seán MacEntee, who was minister from 1941 until 1948, in the UCD Archives. These have not yet been fully catalogued, but Seamus Helferty of the Archives kindly sought out material for me. However, nothing of relevance to this article came to light. Most of the papers of that period appeared to relate to health questions.

II
CITY AND COUNTY MANAGERS SUCCESSION LIST 1929-1990

Joseph Boland and James O'Donnell

This list of holders of the offices of city manager and county manager is intended to provide a chronological structure for all the cities and counties since the appointment of the first Cork city manager in 1929.

The management system was introduced to the county borough corporations as follows: Cork in 1929, Dublin in 1930, Limerick in 1934, Waterford in 1939, and Galway in 1986 (consequent on the constitution of Galway borough as a county borough under the Local Government [Reorganisation] Act 1985). The management system was introduced to the county councils (and urban authorities within the counties) in 1942.

Since 1942, the offices of Dublin City Manager and Dublin County Manager have been held by a single officer. Since 1986, the offices of Galway City Manager and Galway County Manager have been held by the same officer.

Certain counties were originally grouped for county management purposes, with one manager for each group, as follows: Carlow and Kildare, Kilkenny and Waterford, Laois and Offaly, Leitrim and Sligo, Longford and Westmeath, Tipperary North Riding and Tipperary South Riding. They have all since been degrouped — in 1975, 1965, 1982, 1976, 1977 and 1969 respectively. Each of the administrative counties (other than Dublin and Galway) has now a separate manager, as can be seen from the listing.

Those appointed to the offices in a permanent capacity only are listed. It is appropriate, however, to record that the following persons who did not come to hold an office of manager in a permanent capacity did hold office in a temporary capacity for a period in excess of two years — Denis Blackwell (Clare, 1948-52), Patrick Clayton (Cork city, 1970-74), Sean Hayes (Cork county, 1979-81), John P. Keane (Dublin city and county, 1955-58) and Laurence O'Mahoney (Longford, 1975-77).

The City Management Acts and the County Management Act provided that the manager would hold office until he died, resigned or was removed from office. The Local Government Act 1941 empowered the Minister to declare an age limit for all officers. The subsequent application of an age-limit of sixty-five to managers was legally challenged. The legal position was not finally clarified until the enactment of the Local Government Act 1958, which specifically repealed the tenures given by the City Management Acts and the County

Management Act. Some of the earlier managers accordingly had permanent service beyond the age of sixty-five.

The Local Government (Dublin) Act 1930 provided for the creation of an office of borough manager for the newly established corporation of Dun Laoghaire. Following the coming into operation of the County Management Act 1940 on 26 August 1942, the Dublin County Manager became the manager for Dun Laoghaire Corporation. There were two borough managers — Patrick J. Hernon (1930-37) and Timothy C. O'Mahony (1938-42).

Cities

CORK

1929-58	Philip Monahan
1959-70	Walter MacEvilly
1970-74	Vacant
1974-86	Thomas J. McHugh
1987-	Thomas P. Rice

DUBLIN

1930-36	Gerald J. Sherlock
1937-55	Patrick J. Hernon
1955-58	Vacant
1958-65	Timothy C. O'Mahony
1965-76	Matthew Macken
1976-70	James B. Molloy
1979-	Francis J. Feely

GALWAY

1986-	Seamus Keating

LIMERICK

1934-35	Vacant
1936-38	Timothy C. O'Mahony
1939-44	James J. Berkery
1944-46	Vacant
1946-59	Matthew Macken
1959-82	Tomas P. MacDiarmada
1983-87	Thomas P. Rice
1987-	John J. Higgins

WATERFORD

1939-40	Vacant
1940-43	Denis A. Hegarty
1943-45	Vacant
1945-59	Liam Raftis
1959-66	Sean O Giollain
1967-72	John F. Cassidy
1972-75	Vacant
1975-	Michael J. Doody

Counties

CARLOW

1942-44	Edmond A. Joyce
1945-57	Joseph O'Doherty
1958-59	Vacant
1959-65	Matthew Macken
1966-74	Edward M. Murray
1975-89	Michael J. Boyce
1990-	Matthew J. O'Connor

CAVAN

1942-45	Michael A. Veale
1946-71	Dermot McCarthy
1972-87	John F. Cassidy
1988-89	David Mackey
1989-	Brian Johnston

23

CLARE

1942-48	David O'Keeffe
1948-52	Vacant
1952-54	Thomas F. Broe
1954-59	Walter MacEvilly
1960-83	Joseph Boland
1984-	Michael J. Nunan

CORK

1942-54	Joseph F. Wrenne
1954-60	Eugene Callanan
1960-78	Michael N. Conlon
1979-81	Vacant
1981-	Patrick Dowd

DONEGAL

1942-57	Sean D. MacLochlainn
1958-80	Desmond Williams
1980-82	Vacant
1982	Sean P. MacCarthy
1983-	Francis Moloney

DUBLIN

1942-55	Patrick J. Hernon
1955-58	Vacant
1958-65	Timothy C. O'Mahony
1965-76	Matthew Macken
1976-79	James B. Molloy
1979-	Francis J. Feely

GALWAY

1942-65	Clement I. O'Flynn
1966-72	Austin A. Sharkey
1973-	Seamus Keating

KERRY

1942-58	William F. Quinlan
1959-68	Patrick O'Halloran
1968-70	Vacant
1970-73	Seamus Keating
1974-	Thomas F. Collins

KILDARE

1942-44	Edmond A. Joyce
1945-57	Joseph O'Doherty
1958-59	Vacant
1959-65	Matthew Macken
1966-74	Edward M. Murray
1975-	John G. Ward

KILKENNY

1942-64	Simon J. Moynihan
1964-66	Vacant
1966-75	Denis F. Donovan
1976-	Patrick J. Donnelly

LAOIS

1942-45	Patrick J. Bartley
1945-57	Michael A. Veale
1958-66	Edward M. Murray
1966-67	Vacant
1968-81	Patrick Dowd
1981-83	Vacant
1983-	Michael Deigan

LEITRIM

1942-43	Vacant
1943-46	Denis A. Hegarty
1947-58	Denis M. Candy
1959-76	Thomas J. McManus
1976-78	Vacant
1978-	Patrick J. Doyle

LIMERICK

1942-61	Patrick J. Meghen
1961-62	Vacant
1963-69	Thomas M. O'Connor
1970-88	Richard B. Haslam
1989-	Patrick J. Murphy

24

LONGFORD

1942-43	Thomas A. Hayes
1944-69	Michael G. McGeeney
1970-75	Michael J. Boyce
1975-77	Vacant
1978-	Michael J. Killeen

LOUTH

1942-43	Daniel C. Murphy
1944-50	Edmond A. Joyce
1950-52	Vacant
1952-76	James L. MacKell
1977-87	Patrick Lavin
1988-	John Quinlivan

MAYO

1942-44	Michael J. Egan
1944-70	Liam MacLochlainn
1971-75	John G. Ward
1976-89	Michael J. O'Malley
1990-	Desmond P. Mahon

MEATH

1942-43	James Hurley
1944-47	Dermot C. Lawlor
1948-57	Ruairí O Brolchain
1958-71	Denis M. Candy
1971-72	Vacant
1973-75-	Austin A. Sharkey
1976-	Francis J. O'Brien

MONAGHAN

1942-47	Peter McGeough
1947-75	George Cannon
1975-77	Patrick Lavin
1977-	Joseph O. Gavin

OFFALY

1942-45	Patrick J. Bartley
1945-57	Michael A. Veale
1958-66	Edward M. Murray
1966-67	Vacant
1968-81	Patrick Dowd
1982-	Sean P. MacCarthy

ROSCOMMON

1942-65	John G. Browne
1966-74	Sean O Giollain
1975-77	Paul A. Byrne
1978-83	Michael Deigan
1983-84	Michael J. Nunan
1985-	Donal Connolly

SLIGO

1942-43	Vacant
1943-46	Denis A. Hegarty
1947-58	Denis M. Candy
1959-76	Thomas J. McManus
1977-	Paul A. Byrne

TIPPERARY NORTH RIDING

1942-63	John P. Flynn
1964-69	Padraig de Buitleir
1970-77	Thomas Brophy
1978-	John McGinley

TIPPERARY SOUTH RIDING

1942-63	John P. Flynn
1964-69	Padraig de Buitleir
1970-75	Robert N. Hayes
1976-83	Thomas P. Rice
1984-	Seamus Hayes

WATERFORD

1942-64	Simon J. Moynihan
1964-66	Vacant
1966-79	Cathal O Conchubhair
1980-	Daniel Hurley

WESTMEATH

1942-43	Thomas A. Hayes
1944-69	Michael G. McGeeney
1970-75	Michael J. Boyce
1975-77	Vacant
1978-80	Daniel Hurley
1981-	John A. Taaffe

WEXFORD

1942-53	Thomas D. Sinnott
1954-75	Thomas F. Broe
1976-	Michael N. Dillon

WICKLOW

1942-45	Patrick T. Healy
1945-73	Michael Flannery
1973-76	Francis J. O'Brien
1977-84	Seamus Hayes
1985-	Blaise Treacy

III
THE CONTRIBUTION OF THE MANAGEMENT SYSTEM TO LOCAL AND NATIONAL DEVELOPMENT

Michael J. Bannon

The author acknowledges the assistance of Jonathan Tarbatt in the compilation of material for this section.

27

Introduction

The City and County Management system was introduced throughout Irish local government from 1929 onwards. It has coincided with sixty years of dramatic change, modernisation, and development throughout Irish society. During this period, Ireland has been transformed from an agricultural and rural society to an urbanised, industrial and service economy. These changes have, for the most part, taken place within a framework of structures and institutions which the new state inherited, and many of which have remained unreformed. While much has been achieved, it has been argued that the national economic performance has been weak relative to that of our European counterparts (Kennedy, 1988), that we have underachieved because as a society we failed to innovate for our needs, and because we have relied upon the imitation of foreign and often inappropriate models (Lee, 1989). At least in the early years, Ireland's performance may also have been constrained by the fact that the Irish revolutionaries had a distaste for ideology and for social planning. Thus, they were predisposed to accept existing structures and institutions (Akenson, 1975). This was certainly the case with respect to Irish local government where 'the revolutionary of today proved to be the conservative of tomorrow.' In addition, while local government bodies played a significant role in Ireland's struggle for national independence, the tendency to become embroiled in national issues was one of the reasons why in the new state both the number of local authorities and their powers were quickly curtailed.

One of the relatively few exceptions to this general pattern of conservatism was the adoption of the system of city and county management, whose origins have been discussed above, and which has been described as 'perhaps Ireland's major invention in the field of local government' (Chubb, 1964). It is one of the ironies of modern Irish history that the managerial system was so successfully grafted on to an unreformed local government framework, that the noted historian F.S.L. Lyons could claim that if local 'government gained in maturity and competence over the years, then the "managerial revolution" may take a large part of the credit' (Lyons, 1971). This chapter explores some aspects of the growing role of managers over the years, having regard to their statutory and 'basic' functions within the local government system, and also more generally with respect to their 'attached' functions as members of official bodies, coordinating groups, committees and voluntary associations. The chapter is divided into four sections. The first section, 'Ireland 1930-1990: some perspectives on change', provides a brief overview of how the country and society has changed since 1930 and the realities of development since then. The second section looks briefly at the evolution of the local authorities over the past half century, under the heading of 'Changing role and functions of local authorities'. Section three looks at 'The management system within local authorities', while section four is devoted to an overview of the 'The attached functions of the manager' in the local authority system.

Ireland 1930-1990: some perspectives on change

The period from 1930 to 1990 encompasses many variations in economic, social, and political performance. However, in this context we are concerned with the broad parameters of change which set the context

Figure 1: **GNP and central government expenditure, 1948-84 (National Income and Expenditure Tables, CSO) after Brunt.**

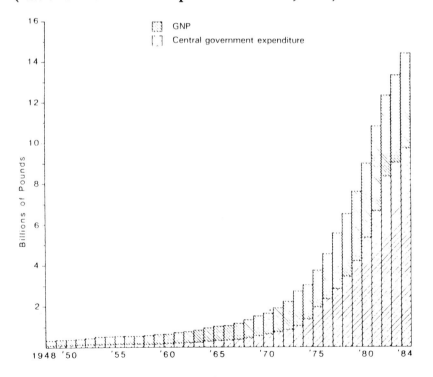

within which the managers were to adopt an increasingly development-oriented role.

Perhaps the best indicator of real change in Ireland has been the growth in GNP, which, while low by many European standards, has underpinned much of the social and economic change which has occurred. Bearing in mind that the index of GNP was unchanged in 1948 from its 1930 level, Figure 1 provides an indication of the overall scale of growth. Table 1 links the growth in GNP to the increasing levels of fixed investment which have risen from 12.6 per cent of GNP in 1938, to 29.2 per cent in the mid 1980s.

TABLE 1: Average annual volume of fixed investments at 1980 constant prices and the average ratio of fixed investment to GNP 1938-85

	1938	'38-46	'47-51	'52-59	'60-73	'74-79	'80-85
Av. annual volume of investment (£m)	383	205	450	603	1200	2174	2626
Av. ratio of fixed investment to GNP at market prices %	12.6	n.a	13.2	16.0	21.4	27.1	29.2

Likewise, over the same period, public capital expenditure has grown six-fold, as seen in Table 2 (Kennedy, 1988) and Figure 1 (Brunt, 1988). Here we can see a corresponding growth in government expenditure alongside the growth of GNP, particularly after 1970. Perhaps nowhere has increased capital investment been more noticeable than in the case of housing, where the total number of dwellings has increased by one third. Overcrowding and obsolescence have been greatly reduced, basic facilities have been vastly increased, and local authorities have played

TABLE 2: Public capital expenditure (at 1980 constant prices), 1933-84

Period	Av. annual Volume £m	Av. share of total investment	Av.annual rate of change
1933-37	251	n.a	13.3
1949-54	327	56.1	4.1
1955-59	296	50.2	-3.3
1960-64	364	46.9	9.6
1965-69	552	45.7	10.1
1970-74	801	45.5	8.8
1975-79	1228	55.6	7.1
1980-84	1510	56.8	0.6

a crucial role in the planning, development, and maintenance of the
stock (Figure 2 (NESC, 1988)). Thus in 1926 there were 584,000 housing
units in the country, a sizable proportion of which were in a poor state
of repair. By 1981, there were 896,000 private dwellings in the country.
In the years 1981 to 1989 inclusive, a total of 205,570 new houses were
erected.

Figure 2: **New house building in Ireland, 1948-85 (*Quarterly
Bulletin of Housing Statistics*, 1970-85, and *Annual Abstract of
Statistics*, 1948-70).**

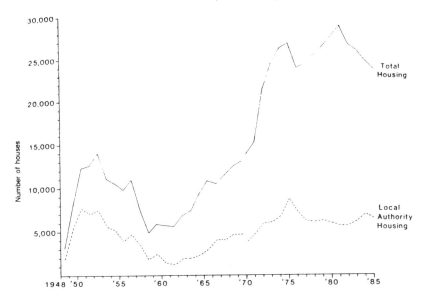

The growth in national production and the corresponding increased
levels of capital investment and public expenditure have required
radically improved management procedures in all branches of the
economy, public and private. While there was a severe reduction in
the public capital programme in the late 1980s, this decline has now
been reversed largely as a consequence of the capital programme of
funding under the Community Support Framework.

The growth in levels of national income masks a dramatic change
in the origin of that production as regards sectoral activity. From being
an agricultural economy, Ireland is now one where almost sixty per cent

31

of GDP originates in the service sector — a change mirrored in the employment shares as set out in Table 3.

TABLE 3: Employment by sector of economic activity, 1926-88 (%)			
Year	Agriculture	Industry	Service
1926	53.5	12.9	33.6
1946	46.8	16.9	36.3
1966	31.3	27.6	41.1
1988	15.2	27.5	57.3

Between 1926 and 1990, almost half a million jobs were lost from agriculture. Industrial employment doubled, and employment in the service sector increased by 50 per cent — an increase of just over 200,000 jobs. These major changes in the sectoral composition of employment are paralleled by comparable changes within occupational groupings. There is an emphasis upon increased skill levels. The changes in the nature of work also reflect a shift in the location of work towards the east of the country, and from rural occupations to urban based trades and professions. The changes also reveal a decline in the total number of persons at work, although there has been a parallel growth in the labour-force. These changes have direct consequences for the operations and activities of local authorities and their managers. By way of example of this process we may cite the case of local authorities themselves where the numbers of unskilled and semi-skilled manual employees have been drastically reduced while the professional and administrative workforce has grown substantially. When the managerial 'system' was introduced, some 28.7 per cent of the total population lived in Connacht-Ulster; by 1988, the share of total population in these counties had fallen to 18.9 per cent. On the other hand, the east region's share of total population had increased from 30.0 per cent of total population in 1951 to 37.7 per cent in 1988. These overall changes have taken place against a backdrop of large-scale emigration in most decades, and a general shift of population from rural to urban environments. Thus, the urban share of population has increased from 37 per cent of total in 1936, to approximately 58 per cent in 1988 — an increase of one million people residing in the 'aggregate urban' areas of the country. The Dublin agglomeration has attracted the lion's share of this growth, with the population of the Dublin 'sub-region' having grown by 427,000 between

32

Figure 3: **National and Dublin population change, 1901-86**

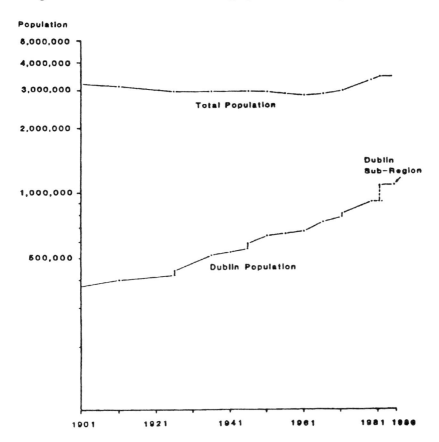

1936 and 1988 — an increase of 72.7 per cent, Figure 3 (Hourihan,
1991). As a consequence, Dublin has come to dominate the national
demographic picture to a much greater extent than in the 1920s (Bannon,
1983; McKeown, 1986; Hourihan, 1991).

Since the inception of the managerial system, Ireland has become a
vastly more wealthy and comfortable society, at least for the majority
of the population. The country has been transformed from an agricultural
and rural based economy into a post-industrial, urban society with a
high dependence upon external communications and an open economy.
In the remaining sections of this chapter an attempt will be made to
explore the role of local authorities and their managers in the overall

processes of change and development. But perhaps nothing so epitomises the nature of change as much as housing. Fifty years ago, the dominant concern was to eliminate unfitness and to remove unsightly and derelict ruins from the landscape. Thus, in 1926, some 27.2 'Persons in Families' were living at an occupancy rate of more than two persons per room and, as recently as 1946, almost half of private dwellings in the country lacked sanitary facilities. While both the local authorities and Bord Fáilte did much to encourage the clearance of derelict houses and ruins from the landscape, there is now considerable concern with the visual intrusion into the landscape caused by modern, fully-serviced, one-off housing, a good deal of which is generated by demand from urban workers. Thus, during the period from 1980 to around 1988, 'one-off' constructions, not all of which were in rural areas, exceeded the total number of new housing units being built in estates. Despite the existence of valuable guidelines, such as Geoghegan's *Building sensitively in the landscapes of Co. Wexford* (1988), a recent survey by Bord Fáilte of bungalow developments in the west of Ireland found that 'Bungalow Blight was rampant', and that '95 per cent of what was regarded as bad development, with very poor design and siting standards, had been authorised without any section four "intervention".' In short, housing in the landscape was still a problem, albeit a very different one from that of the 1930s.

Changing role and functions of local authorities

Within the context of the changes in society outlined above, it has fallen to local authorities to manage many of these changes or to respond to their consequences. The changing role of local authorities may be discussed under a number of different headings, all of which have implications for the role and status of the manager. Over time, there has been a huge increase in the expenditures handled by local authorities. Local authority employment has expanded rapidly and, while some functions have become obsolete, many new functions have been acquired. Thus, many of the labour intensive manual and semi-skilled jobs have been replaced by machinery and by technology for the most part. In addition, the nature of work under particular headings can change quickly, as in the case of housing where the 1980s saw a dramatic shift away from local authority house construction towards repair, maintenance and remedial works. Parallel to these ongoing changes, local authorities were taking on new functions, notably in the fields of

34

planning, development, renewal, environmental management and social
assistance. But, by and large, central government has come to exert
greater control and has virtually eliminated discretion within the local
authority system. Above all, at least to date, there has been no significant reform of the structures of local government to correspond with
the broad socio-economic changes outlined above.

TABLE 4: Local Authority Expenditure: Various Years 1930-88 (£m)

Programme Group	1930-31	1950	1990 (est)
1 Housing and Building	—	3,139	227,221
2 Transport and Safety	2,409	6,030	374,339
3 Water Supply and Sewerage	465	2,072	109,359
4 Devlopment Incentives and Control	—	—	25,451
5 Environmental Protection	—	—	123,603
6 Recreation and Amenity	—	—	89,295
7 Ag. Ed. Health/Welfare	3,029	19,752	57,396
8 Miscellaneous	2,916	5,397	63,094
TOTAL	8,819	26,514	1,069,758

Source: DOE. *Returns of local taxation.* Stationery Office: Dublin

Table 4 serves to provide a broad indication of both the changing scale
of local authority expenditure and the variation in expenditure headings
over time. Thus, in global terms, expenditure has gone up from a mere
£9 million in 1930-31 to over £1 billion in 1990. In the early years before
World War II, the programme of local authority social housing construction had barely begun, and programmes such as Environmental
Protection or Development were unheard of. By the late 1980s, the
'Housing and Building' and 'Road Transportation and Safety'
programmes, accounted for three-quarters of expenditure by local
authorities. By 1990, expenditures on 'Development Incentives and
Control', and 'Environmental Protection/Recreation and Amenity', had
increased to £238 million.

These figures also conceal major changes in functions over time. By
the late 1980s, housing expenditure was almost entirely on maintenance
as compared to the construction programmes of previous decades. The
health function had been transferred to health boards from 1 April 1971,
and most of the concerns relating to agricultural expenditures had
likewise been centralised in regional bodies. There is now much less

emphasis on such operations as drainage works or on contributing to the costs of OPW drainage schemes. However, the local authorities continue to have a very wide range of involvements in such diverse activities as the inspection of abattoirs, overseeing milk and dairy works, the inspection of meat and the regulation of sheep dipping. At the same time, some functions such as school attendance inspections are undertaken only by some local authorities. Others, such as the maintenance of court houses, are undertaken on behalf of the Department of Justice but currently at the expense of the local authorities. In addition, there was an increasing tendency for the funding of many aspects of infrastructural developments to have been targeted for specific schemes on the basis of approvals from the Department of the Environment. Many local authorities, while implementing major schemes of public works, had little or no discretionary funding at their disposal. It is hardly surprising that an examination of the agenda and minutes of council meetings over the past forty years reveals a general continuity, and little change in the role of members. Many reflect a dominant concern with local details and a virtual absence of a focus upon strategic issues.

The increased expenditures by local authorities in general tend to hide the reality that local government was unreformed and seriously obsolete in many respects. The diminishing range of functions directly under local authority control stands in stark contrast to the situation in most of Europe (Council of Europe, 1985). Likewise, the tendency to eliminate discretion in the use of funding tends to run counter to the European norm, particularly outside these islands. Fearful of the growing tendency towards centralisation as early as 1924, Thomas Johnson argued that 'we have to make up our minds whether we want a centralised administration, or whether we want to encourage local authorities to bear responsibility' (Dáil Debates on Local Government Bill, 1924). Writing a quarter century later, Garvin succinctly summed up the reality of Irish local government as a 'process at work: the gathering of control to the centre, the formulation, as a result of the experience gained in the exercise of that control, of certain general rules, and then the devolution to local authorities of full freedom of action within those rules' (Garvin, 1949). A quarter century later the 'full freedom' was replaced by strict controls as the abolition of domestic rates severely undermined local autonomy.

On the structures side, there has been a serious failure to relate local

administrative areas to urban realities, or to alter them in response to
migration or emigration. Instead, we have clung on to the basic unit
of the 1898 legislation, the county, which 'is not a natural division and,
if we have regard to difference in size, wealth and population, not a
rational division' (Collins, 1953-4).

In the absence of any significant reforms of local authorities in terms
of powers, finances, jurisdictions, or the executive role of members,
the introduction of the managerial system was a major innovation. It
is an open question whether local government, as it was known in
Ireland, could have survived at all without the management system,
or whether the unreformed and centrally controlled local authority
system has served to reinforce the role and standing of the city and county
managers.

The management system within local authorities

The introduction of the management system was a profound shock for
Irish local politicians, and one that was deeply resented in many
instances. Debate over the role of managers and their powers vis-à-vis
elected representatives continued until the enactment of the City and
County Management (Amendment) Act, 1955, which 'restored the
position of councils vis-à-vis managers and brought the two into some
sort of equipoise' (Roche, 1982). A possible exception to this is the use
of Section 4 motions to require the manager to make certain planning
decisions, possibly at variance with the policy of the Development Plan
or the technical advice available to the manager.

The early years were inevitably difficult for managers and their hold
on power was rather tenuous. Staffing such a large number of county
and city posts would have posed a strain on even larger and more
developed economies. In the larger authorities, particularly in the urban
ones, the managerial system was imposed on an established system of
strong committees which had to be handled with discretion. But most
of all, in an economy suffering the consequences of an economic war
and the wider impact of a world war, and where there had been little
or no economic growth from 1928 through to 1958, the role of the
manager was inevitably limited and the scope for development was
indeed minimal. Writing in 1944, the then Sligo-Leitrim county manager
saw the new managerial system 'as rationalising democracy in local
government ... the beginning of a great experiment ... in which the

managers must be given time to remodel their organisations on a more modern basis' (Hegarty, 1944). It was an experiment which was to gather speed after 1960, thirty years after its initiation (Collins, 1987).

The post-war era, with the move towards rational management of the public service, began to lay the framework for the leading role of managers in the guiding of growth and in the stimulation of development. The establishment of capital investment programming, the move towards economic planning, and the introduction of economic programming, all served to reinforce the need for good technical management at every level of the public service. Whitaker's *Economic Development* set the agenda for productive investment and the role to be played by the public sector 'since private development has been so limited up to the present'.

Rather quickly thereafter, Lemass sought to generate a fresh approach to the role of public bodies with regard to economic development (Lemass, 1961). He advocated strongly that government departments, state companies, and local authorities should transform themselves into 'development corporations'. For local authorities, the key instrument in this process of transformation was to be the Local Government (Planning and Development) Act, 1963, with its emphasis upon development within a framework of continuing five-year development plans. These required a strong element of strategic thinking, and embraced virtually every facet of economic activity within the jurisdiction of the particular authority (Bannon, 1989). The planning process placed a priority on 'a total development' approach. The local authority and the manager were thus involved in every significant investment decision for their area. Even state authorities were required under Section 84 to 'consult' with the planning authority before proceeding with their developments. The planning process clearly enabled local authorities to function as much more than just the providers of local infrastructure services. They were moving towards the concept of development corporations. The planning process also required a minimum five-year time horizon which enabled strategic thinking on the part of managers and which was also to change the perceptions of councillors and members of authorities about the role of their authorities in the development process.

Perhaps the single most innovative section of the Local Government (Planning and Development) Act of 1963 was Section 77 under which 'a planning authority may develop or secure the development of land

and, in particular and without prejudice to the generality of the fore-
going,' may:
- secure, facilitate and control the improvement of the frontage of any
  public road by widening, opening, enlarging or otherwise improving;
- develop any land in the vicinity of any road or bridge which it is
  proposed to improve or construct;
- provide areas with roads and such services and works as may be
  needed for development;
- provide areas of convenient shape for development;
- secure or carry out, as respects obsolete areas, the development or
  renewal thereof and the provision therein of open spaces;
- secure the preservation of any view or prospect, any structure or
  natural physical feature, any trees subject to a tree preservation order,
  any site of geological, ecological or archaeological interest or any
  flora or fauna subject to a conservation order.

This section also enabled planning authorities to provide sites for
industries and businesses and such other structures and ancillary services
as may be deemed appropriate for the promotion of development.

While these powers were innovative, the planning authorities were
not given the financial resources to make full use of Section 77 and,
as a result, the emergence of local authorities as development corporations
did not take place as quickly or on the lines advocated by the Taoiseach,
Seán Lemass, and his Ministers for Local Government. Nevertheless,
the 1963 Planning Act was to strengthen greatly the strategic role of
the manager, both in respect to the management of resources, and in
the execution of the 'non-reserved' functions as laid down under the
act. Many, including the then Limerick county manager, saw that 'Local
Government clearly has a vital part to play in community development',
and that its role could be enhanced by the new powers offered by the
1963 act (O'Connor, 1963).

The development role of local authorities was enunciated and advanced
throughout the 1960s, and received its clearest definition in the 1971
White Paper on *Local Government Reorganisation*, where it was stated
bluntly that 'Local Authorities, therefore, must now regard themselves
and be regarded as development corporations for their areas. Their
actions reach into very many aspects of modern life and they hold the
reins in local development — economic and physical — in critical
ways . . . the stage has now been reached where increasing emphasis

must be placed on the promotion and support of local development.' The Planning Act enabled local authorities, and in particular their managers, to have a much greater role in industrial and commercial development through such means as planning and zoning, land acquisition and site assemblage and the provision of basic infrastructures. The role of local authorities in industrial development is complex and multifaceted, for example in the provision of road access in cases such as Asahi in North Mayo or the provision of a large volume of water supply to the Alcan Plant near Askeaton in County Limerick. More recently it is possible to cite the role of Kildare County Council in attracting the Intel project to Lexilip. Even in the case of major public sector projects, such as Moneypoint and Turlough Hill, local authorities have a complex and detailed involvement. But at the end of the day, it is probably the increasingly complex demands of the planning process which highlight the fundamental significance of the local authorities in the planning system. Perhaps the outstanding example here is the technical demands placed upon Cork County Council to ensure the environmental and social acceptability of the Sandoz chemical project. Since 1963, local authorities have developed an increasingly complex and sophisticated role in development at all stages from planning to post development monitoring and environmental control. Meanwhile the Development Plan became the basic instrument setting out the likely development of the authority.

While much was written about the emergence of a development role, it was perhaps the establishment of the county development teams which gave the concept its fullest expression, at least for the counties in the designated areas. The terms of reference of the county development teams were:

● To foster the economic development of the county by ensuring that the county derives maximum benefits from the existing state grants and incentives.

● To co-ordinate, within the county, the activities of the public service organisations concerned with economic development and to encourage the officials concerned to work together in developing the resources of the county.

● To receive and examine projects presented to the team by business interests and community organisations which would contribute to the economic development of the county.

40

- To seek out worthwhile projects in the county and investigate their possibilities for economic development.
- To examine proposals for grant assistance under the Small Industries Programme of the Industrial Development Authority, and to provide an 'after care' service for all small industries in the county.
- To assist foreign or native industrialists wishing to set up new manufacturing industry in the county.
- To act as a liaison body between state and semi-state departments and local economic interests in fostering the economic development of the area.
- To compile and maintain a pool of information at town and county level in relation to availability of industrial sites, communication and transport services, labour availability, educational and training facilities, the provision of water and sewerage facilities, power supplies, housing accommodation, the financial aids and other facilities available for economic development in the fields of industry, agriculture, fishing, tourism, etc.

County development teams were established by the government in 1965 in the twelve western counties, and later in west Limerick, with the county manager as chairman, together with the chairman of the county council, the county engineer, the county agricultural officer and a number of other local authority officers. Each team appointed a full-time county development officer 'to act as a chief executive for development in the area'. A review of the work of the county development teams over the years 1981 to 1985 concluded that 'when account is taken of the very wide range of activities encompassed by the County Development Teams . . . and the very low cost of jobs created, it is clear that the Western Development Fund represents a very good return on investment.' While county development teams were not established in the 'non-designated' counties initially, these counties did appoint county development officers to assist the county manager in the promotion of development within the county.

The county managers have played a key role in the successful operation of the teams — a role whose importance was quickly recognised. Thus, the *Public Service Organisation Review Group Report* in 1969 pinpointed 'the key role of the County Manager', which it regarded as 'significant in that a local government officer is being used to co-ordinate, locally, national services'. Had the Devlin proposal for a 'super' Department of Regional Development been given effect, then the basic functions of the manager within each local authority would have been greatly enhanced. As it was, most of the reports were advisory or for discussion, but, while they were not given statutory effect, they did indicate the type of role that the managers could and should play. None did this more so that the McKinsey report on *Strengthening the Local Government Service*, which provided a blueprint for the county manager as the head of a management team. The report proposed the appointment of 'Service Managers', which would lead to a change in the role of the county manager, 'to enable him to devote more time to co-ordinating services and planning the development of the county'. The general thrust of the report was aimed at a more efficient local authority service with 'an organisation in each county . . . that is more strongly oriented towards management than towards the traditional professional or technical approaches'. Finally, the report stressed the importance of training for all local authority staff, management included.

While the various reports on the reform of the local government system were not implemented, they did have two direct implications for the role of the manager in the discharge of the basic managerial functions. Firstly, these reports, *inter alia*, placed an emphasis upon modern management systems. Greater priority was given to training and the general emphasis upon land use planning had induced a five-year horizon and an overall strategic approach. Secondly, by virtue of the fact that Irish local government was not reformed, that councillors remained part-time and unpaid and that, increasingly, key decisions had to have the sanction of the Department of the Environment, the manager was placed in a relatively stronger position. Again, to quote F.S.L. Lyons, 'These officials were permanent, full-time, well-paid administrators . . . in practice, of course, both because of his expertise and because he enjoyed the priceless advantage of continuity, the Manager, especially if he had the rudiments of tact, was in a position to influence very powerfully the course of local government.'

In this type of power structure, the hand of the manager and the managerial role was strengthened as the functions discharged by local authorities changed over time. Thus, the transfer of the health function from local authorities on 1 April 1971 largely removed from elected members one of their key areas of interest and concern. More recently, the virtual cessation of public housing construction is another case in point. At the same time, the new roles and functions were often technical and operated in close association with the manager on a day-to-day basis. Examples include water pollution control, the development of recreational areas and facilities, the provision of amenities and more recently, in the case of a number of expanding urban centres, the operation of the Urban Renewal Act, 1986. As the affairs of local government became increasingly technical, the role of a continuous, well-equipped and involved management system became more important.

Although it is too soon to see the urban renewal legislation in its longer term perspective, it is likely that this legislation will represent a landmark in the developmental role of local authorities. Section 77 of the Local Government (Planning and Development) Act, 1963 placed an emphasis upon development, but it did not provide adequate financial means to achieve its objectives. The urban renewal legislation, no doubt drawing inspiration from the work led by managers in a number of cities in the 1980s, linked fiscal and taxation incentives to 'designated areas' within the context of the development plans for the areas in question. The result has been a flurry of badly needed investment, particularly in run-down parts of the cities of Galway, Limerick, Waterford, Cork, and more recently in Dublin. Since 1986 the urban renewal process has been an evolving one with extensions to the designated areas in most county boroughs and the designation of areas in other urban centres. Thus, in 1988 parts of nine provincial towns were designated under the act, and a further eight were added to the list in May 1990.

As of July 1990, a total of 218 projects with a capital value of £175 million have been completed or are in progress, while a further 127 projects with an estimated value of £135 million are planned (Table 5).

TABLE 5: Urban Renewal Programme Summary 1/7/90. Total Value of Projects (£000s)

	Completed	Progress	Planning	Total
The Five County Boroughs	45,821	75,770	86,570	208,161
Nine Provincial Towns	5,956	3,218	41,819	50,993
Tallaght Town Centre	420	45,500	7,110	53,030
Total	52,197	124,488	135,499	312,184

While the areas designated under the Urban Renewal Act, 1986 constitute but a small part of the territory of the state, the urban renewal legislation may now be said to justify the word development in the title of the 1963 act. Coming on stream at a time of economic expansion,

43

it has stimulated a wave of urban renewal activity in which the manager has played a key role in securing designation, the assemblage of sites, attracting investors and developers, ensuring the completion of the development, and securing end users for the project. This has involved the bringing together of a wide range of experience and know-how gained by managers, in terms of both their basic functions, and the 'attached' functions acquired over the years, principally over the past twenty to twenty-five years. But perhaps, more than any other act, the urban renewal legislation has established the development function of local authorities with the manager playing a leading developmental role within the authority. Outside the designated areas, local authority managers have also become intricately involved in development. But in this latter case, much of their effort is through their attached functions in support of the work of other agencies and organisations.

The attached functions of the manager
Reference has already been made to the establishment of the county development teams and to the role of the county manager in the co-ordination of national functions. This was a significant landmark in the expansion of the role of managers into areas of development both within and beyond their statutory role as the chief officer of the local authorities.

Somewhat ironically, the failure to implement the development strategy set out in *Regional Studies in Ireland* in 1969 (the Buchanan Report) was to provide a new and greatly enlarged opportunity for managers in the development process throughout Ireland. Effectively rejecting a growth centre strategy, the government established nine Regional Development Organisations, modelled upon that established in the Mid-West Region in 1967, 'to co-ordinate the programmes for development in each region'. The RDOs, both in terms of their management boards and their technical committees, were extremely broadly based, involving all sectors of economic activity and the major development interests from the public sector within each region. In addition, they brought together both the elected members, the managers, and the technical officers of all local authorities within the region. Their objective was to contribute to the fulfilment of national development targets through comprehensive regional development. As Vincent Cullinane summed it up, 'an objective should be to seek to achieve

44

integrated comprehensive strategic planning at both national and regional level' (Cullinane, 1976).

In their eighteen-year existence, the Regional Development Organisations represented a low cost, inexpensive way of integrating development interests within each region. Although they were never given statutory recognition, the RDOs, through their regional reports, regional development plans and sectoral studies, did introduce an element of strategic thinking at the subnational level, and they provided a framework for the co-ordination of local development plans — a framework that increasingly embraced cross border studies. Above all, the work of the RDOs provided a comprehensive picture of the development needs and potentials of each region, together with a schedule of viable development projects across all branches of the economy, and within the remit of a wide diversity of agencies. On the technical side, this work was enhanced by the research inputs of An Foras Forbartha and its Conservation Advisory Service (CAS).

The attached functions of the manager have come to embrace virtually every aspect of development in a modern economy and through these functions the manager has been a comprehensive development officer for the territory of the respective authority. These attached functions may be grouped under a number of interrelated headings:

(a) *Co-operation and interfacing with other state agencies*: The manager as chief officer of the local authority is involved in collaborative and co-operative efforts, often of a joint-venture nature with virtually every arm of government, including the departments of state and the state-sponsored bodies. In undertaking development with the local authority it is necessary in many instances to work hand-in-hand with such agencies as the Industrial Development Authority, Bord Fáilte, FÁS, the ESB, Telecom Éireann and An Bord Pleanála. In certain counties, there is a lengthy record of productive co-operation with Bord na Móna while in other parts of the country the development of forest parks and amenities required close collaboration with the forestry service. More recently, the development of marinas has led to joint efforts by the local authority and the Department of the Marine (as at Kilrush and Dun Laoghaire). Of particular note has been the development of parks and amenities and the restoration of properties in conjunction with the Office of Public Works. One of the more imaginative out-turns of these types of arrangements has been the development of the Kilkenny Civic Trust which has now taken over much of the heritage of Kilkenny city from the OPW. Less formal in nature is the role of the local authority in Meath in promoting with the Office of Public Works the development of The Boyne Valley Archaeological Park. Another widespread example of local authority co-operation has been that with Bord Fáilte to help prepare towns to compete in the Tidy Towns Competition through the undergrounding of cables, the removal of eyesores, the development of town and village amenities and the encouragement of civic pride. An important recent trend has been the involvement of local authorities in the commercial development of some of the big estates and great houses, as at Straffan and Lyons in Kildare.

Finally, local authorities assist and facilitate the operations of a large number of state agencies and their programmes. Examples include assembling sites for government office relocations, maintaining Garda stations and courthouses, as well as accommodating the requirements of services such as Bus Éireann. In short, the local authority manager may be seen as a key actor in the implementation of works covering all aspects of development by or on behalf of state agencies.

(b) *Joint ventures with public and private developers:* These can range from job creation and infrastructure projects through housing developments to amenity and recreation investments. Again, the degree of formality in the arrangements varies from project to project as does the balance of investments. Examples have included the securing of sites for industry, exercising rights of pre-emption to assemble sites for renewal, procuring sites for shopping developments, the development of out-of-town shopping complexes and co-operation with voluntary and co-operative housing groups. An important example of joint ventures in recent years has been the development of local or regional airports as at Knock, Galway, Kerry and Waterford. The local authorities have played a key role in the development of these important commercial and tourism-related initiatives. But perhaps it is in the field of amenity and recreation that some of the finest outcomes of joint venture decisions can be found. Notable examples include the Gartan estate in Donegal, the Craggaunowen visitor centre in Clare, the development of Lakeshore amenities by North Tipperary, and more recently the development of Roscrea as a 'theme town'. There are also further joint proposals from North Tipperary, Clare and Shannon Development to have Ballina-Killaloe recognised within the concept of theme town. Examples of joint

46

ventures are many and varied but undoubtedly amongst the more important must range urban renewal initiatives.

(c) *Urban renewal developments*: Reference has already been made to the work of local authority managers in the field of urban renewal under the Urban Renewal Act, 1986, but the involvement of local authorities in joint renewal ventures is of much longer duration and of wider extent than that taking place under the recent legislation. In fact problems of urban renewal were central to the arguments favouring a new planning act in the early 1960s. Early efforts at urban renewal must include the foresight of many towns to introduce relief roads to take heavy traffic away from town centres. Other examples of urban renewal include the large ILAC centre development of Henry Street in Dublin as well as various other commercial ventures in Dublin. In the case of Dublin, there was also an initiative to promote private house development at Malpas Street as well as a number of instances of transforming derelict sites into amenity parks. Outside Dublin, notably in Cork and Waterford, much was achieved in terms of urban renewal in the 1970s and 1980s, largely as a result of the persuasive powers and foresight of managers and their staffs but also with the support of members. Throughout the country, most towns began to explore the feasibility of developing rational proposals for the better use of town-centre backlands. Much progress was made, as in the case of Carlow, Navan and Portlaoise, where the town centre has been expanded on to such lands. Other towns with evident potential included Dundalk and Longford, to name but two.

Even at the present time it has to be realised that urban renewal is not just confined to either the selected towns or their designated areas. Many schemes of pedestrianisation and civic improvement across the country are at the core of urban revitalisation. An important contribution to urban rehabilitation and improvements, at least in border counties, has come from monies provided by the International Fund for Ireland and which has been used for projects such as the civic improvement of the town centre in Cavan and the pedestrianisation and lighting of the shopping streets in Manorhamilton.

(d) *Cross-border co-operation*: The involvement of the International Fund for Ireland is but one aspect of the growing importance of cross-border co-operation. Local authorities from both sides of the border have co-operated over a long number of years. In the 1970s and 1980s this co-operation led to a large number of studies and reports from which flowed significant cross-border transport and amenity development projects, notably between Derry and Donegal. Here the spirit of co-operation has continued and has expanded into cross-border co-operation in higher education between Magee College in Derry and the Regional Technical College in Letterkenny, involving the latest forms of high quality communications technology. Further south, the Lough Melvin study has resulted in a range of cross-border projects to ensure the greater use of the area's angling and tourist resources. Here, as elsewhere, cross-border co-operation includes joint marketing and The East Region Cross-Border Committee (involving Monaghan and Louth county councils and Newry and Mourne, and Down district councils) is involved in the joint promotion of the sub-region as well as in the development of water supplies, the improvement of transport links, the creation of employment and the study of the feasibility of a local airport. One of the largest projects to flow from cross-border studies such as the Erne Catchment Study, involves the opening of the Ballinamore-Ballyconnell canal, linking the Erne and Shannon navigations. When completed in 1993, this project is expected to greatly improve cross-border tourism links and it is estimated that it will benefit the region by £1.35 million per annum in increased tourism earnings, resulting in benefits of £34.2 million over the lifetime of the canal.

Cross-border co-operation also involves Co-operation North in local library exchange services but of course the operations of Co-operation North are not just confined to the border areas. They include many island-wide projects, such as traditional Irish musical exchanges between Clare and Belfast.

(e) *The implementation of the Community Support Framework*: The cross-border projects, like urban renewal works in the designated towns and cities, have established the manager at local level as a key actor in the achievement of national development policies. It was to be expected that the manager would play, and will continue to play, a key role in relation to Ireland's funding under the EC Community Support Framework, 1989-93. In late 1988 and early 1989, the county managers had a leading role in the sub-regional 'working groups' which prepared and costed the sub-regional inputs into Ireland's National Programme of Community Interest under the revised EC Structural Funding Process, the *National Development Plan, 1989-93*. The subsequent *Community Support Framework* for Ireland agreed a programme of capital expenditure by the EC of £2.86 billion, which will be on the basis of partnership between the EC and the Irish public and private sectors.

The details of the proposed EC expenditures by operational prog-rammes are set out in Table 6 below, with almost all expenditure headings leading to increased capital investment through the local author-ities. In addition other unspecified CSF funding is likely to be available for selected projects, such as the Temple Bar area of inner Dublin.

TABLE 6: EC Community Support Framework Proposed Expenditures 1989-93

	£m	%
Agriculture, fishing, forestry, rural development	524.6	18.3
Tourism	118.	44.1
Sanitary Services	95.0	3.3
Industry & Services	416.0	14.5
Roads	447.1	15.6
Rail and Access Transport	94.3	3.3
Human Resources	1,122.9	39.3
Telecommunications & Postal Services, Energy, Star, Valoren and Non Quota programmes, Technical Assistance	42.1	1.6
Total	2,860.4	100.0

Source: Ireland's Community Support Framework, Brussels, 1989

This programme of investment will be implemented largely at the local level, and will involve the managers in a number of ways. First of all, local managers will be actively involved in the monitoring groups within each sub-region which will comprise the following:

● the chairman and one other member (to be selected by the council concerned of each county council, county borough council and other local authority with a population in excess of 15,000, including environs)

● a representative of each of the following organisations:
  Chambers of Commerce of Ireland
  Confederation of Irish Industry
  Construction Industry Federation
  Federation of Irish Employers
  Irish Congress of Trade Unions (two representatives)
  Irish Co-operative Organisation Society
  Irish Creamery Milk Suppliers' Association
  Irish Farmers' Association
  Macra na Feirme

● the county and city managers of the relevant local authorities

- a representative of each of the following government departments:
  Agriculture and Food
  Environment
  Finance
  Industry and Commerce
  Labour
  Tourism and Transport
- a representative of the EC Commission.

In addition, other departments may be represented. The committees will nominate their own chairman and vice-chairman. The committees are required to meet at least twice yearly, and to monitor the progress of works involving EC funding under the Community Support Framework programmes. Involvement in these sub-regional monitoring committees will give the managers another critical role in the national development process. It is likely that it will frequently fall to them to bring together the necessary local partnerships of public and private interests to ensure that infrastructural, recreational, and job-creating projects get off the ground effectively and efficiently. In this way, the 1990s are likely to see the managers undertaking a wider role of co-ordination and development promotion on behalf of all branches of government. Managers will have a role at local level in the implement-ation process and in ensuring the success of EC and national investments in terms of the local area and for community development.

(f) *Community and local development*: This is another of the attached functions which in many instances proceeds with either the moral or financial assistance of the manager or both. Community development initiatives have been strongest to date in the west of Ireland. Here, local authorities have co-operated with both Udarás na Gaeltachta and Roinn na Gaeltachta in support of co-operative initiatives to foster enterprise and job creation as in the case of the Enterprise Centre in Mullingar. In many instances the local authority can make a project or an event feasible for the community either through the provision of sites or infrastructure or by means of small incentive grants to local groups. Here, the work has very often involved co-operation with ANCO and the YEA (now FÁS), providing community halls and local initiatives which have a significant training content as well as a potential for employment. In addition, many of these had the indirect effect of improving the towns' appearance vis-à-vis the Tidy Town Competition.

A related area of involvement of the local authorities has been with the activities of the Rural Housing Organisation in the west of Ireland and assisting in the improvement of the way of life of rural dwellers through the promotion of, or assistance with, group and local water schemes. Many of these community-based initiatives have served to improve the quality of rural life and to reduce the hardships and the isolation of rural living.

(g) *Involvement in cultural, educational and artistic initiatives:* Much of this work involves the traditional role of the local authorities operating through the vocational education committees and ensuring the provision of libraries and school sites. A more recent addition to this range of activities has been the development of a network of county and local museums which have an educational and touristic role. In many instances, the notion has been taken a great deal further with the development of heritage centres, notably the Irish National Heritage Centre in Wexford and the Heritage Park at Glendalough. These are complemented by an increasing range of visitor centres as at the Aillwee Caves in Clare, or interpretative centres such as the Slieve Bloom interpretative centre in Birr. This concept has now been expanded to include wider geographical areas of historical or scientific interest. Examples include the proposed Clonmacnoise Heritage Zone as well as the peatland interpretative centres at Lullymore in Kildare and Clara in Offaly. More recently, the notion of 'theme towns' has been redefined in terms of 'heritage towns' and a large number has been proposed for designation.

Conclusion

The attached, often non-statutory functions of local authorities, have expanded rapidly in recent years. Since the 1960s, largely in association with the work of the RDOs, the managers became increasingly involved in the development and implementation of a wide range of projects within their county, and have been operative within both the private sector and the higher levels of government.

It is clear that the local authority system is viewed as an effective vehicle for the provision of services and development know-how at local level. In turn, as one manager put it, 'For our part, we must ensure that we do our job efficiently and professionally and having done so continue to improve our public image and our public relations' (Johnston, 1985).

This section has sought to highlight the role of the managerial system in local and national development. The chapter has examined the parameters of change in the Irish economy since the inception of the managerial system, with particular reference to the period since the initiation of economic programming just over a quarter century ago. Against a general background in which the Irish government failed to carry through any significant reform of local government, and in an era when Ireland often opted for 'muddling through', rather than a planned approach, the success of the managerial system is noteworthy. The role of the manager has been consolidated both in terms of the basic functions within the local authorities and, more generally, through 'attached' functions as a manager of development in the area as a whole.

While the success of the manager may, in some instances, derive from personal flair and tact, more generally it arises from the consolidation of the role within the system, from better management training, and from the advantages of continuity and expertise. In any event, the introduction of the management system may be viewed as both a 'major invention', and one of the successes of Irish local government. While the current review of local government structures and functions being carried out by government may lead to some changes in the role of the managers, the management system seems set to play a key role both in community development and in the implementation of national development programmes in the years ahead.

References

Akenson, D.H., *A mirror to Kathleen's face: Education in independent Ireland 1922-60*, McGill-Queens University Press, Montreal, 1975

Bannon, M.J., *Planning: The Irish experience, 1920-1988*, Wolfhound Press, Dublin, 1989

Bannon, M.J., 'Urbanisation in Ireland: growth and regulation' in J. Blackwell and F. Convery (eds), *Promise and performance: Irish environmental policies analysed*, Resource and Environmental Policy Centre, University College, Dublin, 1983, pp261-285

Bannon, M.J. and Tarbatt, J., *Republic of Ireland*, IFHP, The Hague, 1990

Brunt, B., *The Republic of Ireland*, Paul Chapman (Economic and Social Series), London, 1988

Chubb, B.(Editor), *A source book of Irish government*, IPA, Dublin, 1964

Collins, J., 'The evolution of county government' *Administration*, Vol.1, 1953-4, pp79-88

Collins, N., *Local government managers at work*, IPA, Dublin, 1987

Council of Europe, *Management structures in local and regional government*, Strasbourg, 1985

Cullinane, V., 'Framework for Regional Development: the RDO Viewpoint', *Administration*, Vol.24, 1976, p322

Daly, M.E., *Social and economic history of Ireland since 1800*, Educational Co, Dublin, 1981

Garvin, J., 'Nature and extent of control over local government system' in F.C. King, *Public administration in Ireland,* Parkside Press, Dublin, 1949, pp162-173

Hegarty, D.A., 'An outline of local government administration' in *Public administration in Ireland,* Vol.1, Parkside Press, Dublin, 1944, pp145-160

Hourihan, K., 'Culture, politics and recent urbanisation in the Republic of Ireland' in M.J. Bannon et al. (eds), *Urbanization and urban development: recent trends and strategies in a global context,* Dublin, 1991.

Johnston, B., 'The role of local authorities in economic and employment development — the Irish Experience', in *Proceedings of annual conference,* General Council of County Councils, 1985, pp 23-26

Kennedy, K.A., *The economic development of Ireland in the twentieth century,* Routledge: London, 1988

Lemass, S.F.,., 'The organisation behind the economic programme', *Administration,* Vol. 9, 1961, pp 3-10

Lee, J., *Ireland: 1912-1985 politics and society,* CUP, Cambridge, 1989

Lyons, F.S.L., *Ireland since the famine,* Collins/Fontana, London, 1971

McKeown, K., 'Urbanisation in the Republic of Ireland: a conflict approach', in P. Clancy et al. (eds.), *Ireland: A sociological profile,* IPA, Dublin, 1986, pp 362-379

National Economic and Social Council, *A review of housing policy,* NESC No.87, Stationery Office, Dublin, 1988

O'Connor.T., 'Local government and community development', *Administration,* Vol.11, 1963, pp296-310

Returns of Local Taxation, DOE, Stationery Office, Dublin, various years.

Roche, D., *Local government in Ireland,* IPA, Dublin, 1982.

IV
CITY AND COUNTY MANAGERS
1929-1990
CAREER PROFILES

Joseph Boland and James O'Donnell

55

Ninety-three persons were appointed in a permanent capacity to the office of city manager or county manager in this period. Two — Philip Monahan and Gerald J. Sherlock — were appointed by statute. All the others were appointed on the recommendation of the Local Appointments Commissioners.

Extensive research and inquiries were undertaken to establish facts and dates and to ensure that as complete a career profile as possible could be constructed for each manager. We thank all who facilitated and assisted us in this. The vital assistance from the Local Appointments Commission has already been acknowledged in the preface but we must again express our thanks here and, in particular, to the Secretary, Brendan Lannon, and Howard Moorehead and Pat O'Dea of the Commission's staff. Without the records and information that they made available to us it would scarcely have been possible to construct career profiles of very many of the managers.

In general, only substantive posts held are included in the profiles. Many managers, however, were from time to time during their careers in higher posts in a temporary capacity, including posts as county manager. The only temporary higher posts included are those where the tenure was of exceptional duration or where the temporary post was by way of secondment to another authority or where a manager, immediately preceding his appointment as a manager in a permanent capacity, had been manager in a temporary capacity in the same city or county.

Apart from their statutory responsibilities, managers have been involved in a number of ancillary or cognate organisations. Such *ex officio* involvements are not included in the profiles.

In July 1940, in exercise of powers under the Emergency Powers Act, 1939, the Minister for Supplies appointed a senior local officer in each county (other than Dublin) as county commissioner, with contingent powers and responsibilities. The officers appointed included city managers, commissioners for dissolved local authorities, secretaries of county councils, secretaries of boards of health and public assistance and county registrars. From August 1942 until the end of the Emergency in 1945 the county manager was appointed the county commissioner (except where the city manager had been the commissioner). Accordingly, appointment as county commissioner is shown in the profiles only for the period 1940 to 1942. The radio broadcast made on 19 July 1940 by Seán Lemass, TD, Minister for Supplies, on the appointment of the Emergency Commissioners, is given in appendix 2.

BARTLEY, Patrick J. (1878-1948)

Born County Cavan

In business, 1891-98
Farmer and journalist, 1899-1908

Clerk, Oldcastle Board of Guardians, 1908-22

Inspector, Department of Local Government and Public Health, 1922-30

Commissioner, Mayo County Council and Mayo Board of Health and
Public Assistance, 1931-32
Commissioner, Galway Board of Health and Public Assistance, 1931-32

Inspector, Department of Local Government and Public Health, 1932-34

Commissioner, Laoighis County Council and Laoighis Board of Health
and Public Assistance, 1934-42
Commissioner, Westmeath County Council and Westmeath Board of
Health and Public Assistance, 1935-42

County Commissioner, Laoighis, 1940-42

Laoighis-Offaly County Manager, 1942-45

In 1902, Mr Bartley founded (with four others), managed and edited
Sinn Fein, a monthly review printed in Oldcastle. Arthur Griffith,
writing in the 4 July 1902 issue of *The United Irishman*,
of which he was editor, commented:

The first number of *Sinn Fein*, a monthly review edited in Oldcastle and
printed with Irish ink on Irish paper, has reached us. *Sinn Fein* is
another sign of how the intellectual life of the country has quickened.

BERKERY, James J. (1892-1980)

Born Limerick city

Associate of the Corporation of Registered Accountants (1917)
Fellow of the Institute of Company Accountants (1938)
Fellow of the Faculty of Secretaries (1938)

Employed in Accountant's Office, Great Southern Railways, 1909-13

Employed in the City Accountant's Department, Dublin Corporation, 1913-17
Accountancy and Secretarial work, Land Cultivation Department, Dublin Corporation, 1917-20
Secretary, Re-organisation Committee, Dublin Corporation, 1920-21
Town Clerk, Clonmel Corporation, 1921-39

Limerick City Manager, 1939-44

County Commissioner, Limerick, 1940-42

BOLAND, Joseph (1922-   )

Born County Kerry

BComm (UCD, 1943)
BA and Diploma in Public Administration (UCD, 1944)

Temporary Town Clerk, Listowel UDC, 1945-46
Town Clerk, Listowel UDC, 1946-48
Staff Officer, Westmeath County Council, 1948-49
County Accountant, Offaly County Council, 1949-54
County Secretary, Carlow County Council, 1954-60

Clare County Manager, 1960-83

Chairman, Lisdoonvarna Failte Ltd, 1967-83
Trustee, Clare Social Service Council, 1968-83
Member, National Social Service Council (since 1984 the National Social Service Board), 1971-74
Director, Craggaunowen Project, 1972-83
Chairman, County and City Managers' Association, 1972-75
Director, Rent-an-Irish Cottage Ltd, 1976-78
Chairman, Local Government Staff Negotiations Board, 1977-78
Director, National Building Agency Ltd, 1977-83

Adviser, Conference of the Peripheral Maritime Regions of the EEC, 1983-
Director, Craggaunowen Project, 1984-
Director, Syntex Ireland Ltd, 1984-
Member, Public Library Service Review Group, 1986-87
Chairman, An Chomhairle Leabharlanna, 1988-

Inaugural meeting of the County Managers' Association held on 20 January 1943: (Front row, l-r) J.P. Flynn, Tipperary (N.R.) & (S.R.), D.C. Murphy, Louth, W.F. Quinlan, Kerry, E.A. Joyce, Carlow/Kildare, P.J. Bartley, Laois/Offaly, P.J. Meghen, Limerick. (Second row, l-r) M.J. Egan, Mayo, C.I. O'Flynn, Galway, J.G. Browne, Roscommon, P.T. Healy, Wicklow. (Third row, l-r) P. McGeough, Monaghan, M.A. Veale, Cavan, S.D. MacLochlainn, Donegal, T. Hayes, Longford/Westmeath, S.J. Moynihan, Kilkenny/Waterford). (Back row, l-r) J.F. Wrenne, Cork, D. O'Keeffe, Clare, J. Hurley, Meath, T.D. Sinnott, Wexford.

BOYCE, Michael J. (1927-)

Born County Donegal

BA (UCD, 1980)

Barrister-at-Law (The King's Inns, Dublin, 1985)

Clerical Officer, Donegal County Council, 1948-53
Assistant Clerk, Cork Mental Hospital Board, 1954
Staff Officer, Louth County Council, 1955-57
Town Clerk, Ennis UDC, 1957-58
Town Clerk, Athlone UDC, 1958-59
County Secretary, Kerry County Council, 1959-62
County Secretary, Leitrim County Council, 1962-66
County Secretary, Meath County Council, 1966-70

Longford-Westmeath County Manager, 1970-75
Carlow County Manager, 1975-89

Director, An Foras Forbartha, 1971-77
Chairman, Local Government Computer Services Board, 1981-82
Chairman, County and City Managers' Association, 1986-88
Member, Industrial Development Authority South East
Region Small Industries Board, 1989

In practice at the Bar, 1989-

BROE, Thomas F. (1910-85)

Born County Kildare

B Comm (UCD,1930)

Audit Clerk, Messrs Kenny & Co., Accountants and Auditors, Dublin, 1930-31
Clerk, and for two years Assistant Cashier, Texaco (Ireland) Ltd, Dublin, 1931-36

Accountant, Kildare Board of Health and Public Assistance, 1936-40
County Accountant, Carlow County Council, 1940-42
County Accountant, Limerick County Council, 1943-44
County Secretary, Kilkenny County Council, 1944-46
County Secretary, Limerick County Council, 1946-52

Clare County Manager, 1952-54
Wexford County Manager, 1954-75

Temporary Wexford County Manager, 1975-76

Chairman, County and City Managers' Association, 1963-64

BROPHY, Thomas (1914-77)

Born County Tipperary

ACCA (1940)

Clerk, Tipperary (NR) Board of Health and Public Assistance, 1936-42
Clerk, Tipperary (NR) County Council, 1942-43
County Accountant, Tipperary (NR) County Council, 1943-57
County Secretary, Tipperary (NR) County Council, 1957-70
(Temporary Tipperary (NR and SR) Assistant County Manager, 1964-69)
(Temporary Tipperary (NR) County Manager, 1969-70)

Tipperary (NR) County Manager, 1970-77

Director, Rent-an-Irish-Cottage Ltd, 1976-77

BROWNE, John G. (1902-76)

Born Dublin city

Temporary Clerk, Galway County Council, Galway UDC and Galway
Board of Guardians, 1919-21
Private Assistant to Town Clerk, Galway UDC, 1922-29
Private Assistant to Secretary, Galway Harbour Commissioners, 1922-35
Rent Collector, Galway UDC, 1924-35
Secretary, Galway Cemeteries Committee, 1927-35
Official Assistant to Town Clerk, Galway UDC, 1929-33
Temporary Secretary, Galway Harbour Commissioners, 1933-34
Temporary Secretary, Galway Harbour Commissioners, 1933-34
Temporary Town Clerk, Galway UDC, 1933-35
Secretary, Laoighis Board of Health and Public Assistance, 1936-41
County Secretary, Longford County Council, 1941-42

Roscommon County Manager, 1942-65

Secretary to various Development Committees in Galway, 1922-35
Secretary, Galway Conjoint Harbour Development Committee, 1928-33
Secretary, Galway Chamber of Commerce, 1928-35

Commissioner, Bray UDC, 1970-73

BYRNE, Paul A. (1932-   )

Born County Longford

Diploma in Social and Economic Science (UCG, 1955)

Clerical Officer, Sligo County Council, 1949-60
Town Clerk, Ceannanus Mor UDC, 1960-62
Staff Officer, Donegal County Council, 1962-68
County Accountant, Donegal County Council, 1968-70
County Secretary, Donegal County Council, 1970-72

Programme Manager, North Western Health Board, 1972-75

Roscommon County Manager, 1975-77
Sligo County Manager, 1977-

Member, The Fire Prevention Council, 1980-82
Member, Irish Water Safety Association, 1981-82
Chairman, Hawk's Well Theatre, Sligo, 1982-
Member, Industrial Development Authority Donegal
and North West Region Small Industries Board, 1985-
Director, Opera Theatre Company, Dublin, 1987-90
Director, North-Western Regional Tourism Organisation Ltd, 1990-

CALLANAN, Eugene (1899-1960)

Born Cork city

Clerical Assistant, Cork County Council, 1924-40
County Accountant and Local Taxation Officer, Cork County Council,
1940-44
County Secretary, Westmeath County Council, 1944-46
County Secretary, Cork County Council, 1947-54

Cork County Manager, 1954-60

CANDY, Denis M. (1906-79)

Born County Kildare

ACCA (1940)
ACIS (1948)

Senior Clerk and Deputy Chief Clerk, Dublin Port and Docks Board, 1927-44

Teacher, Rathmines High School of Commerce (night classes), 1939-44

County Accountant, Roscommon County Council, 1944
County Secretary, Laois County Council, 1944-45
County Secretary, Kildare County Council, 1945-47

Leitrim-Sligo County Manager, 1947-58
Meath County Manager, 1958-71

Temporary Meath County Manager, 1971-72

Member, Commission of Inquiry on Mental Handicap, 1961-65
Chairman, County and City Managers' Association, 1969-72
Chairman, Local Government Staff Negotiations Board, 1971-72

Chairman, National Road Safety Association, 1976-78

CANNON, George (1910-)

Born County Donegal

BA (UCD, 1932)
H Dip in Ed (UCD,1933)

Teacher, Caffrey's College, Dublin (for H Dip in Ed), 1932-33
Private tuitions and articles for press, 1933-34

Temporary Town Clerk, Letterkenny UDC, 1934-35
Town Clerk, Letterkenny UDC, 1935-41
Temporary Town Clerk, Bundoran UDC, 1940-41
Town Clerk, Dundalk UDC, 1941-45
County Secretary, Wexford County Council, 1945-47

Monaghan County Manager, 1947-75

Weekly columnist ('Borderlines'), *Northern Standard*, 1976-79

CASSIDY, John F.(1922-)

Born County Mayo

BComm (UCG, 1944)
H Dip in Ed (UCG, 1945)
DPA (UCD, 1946)
MComm (UCG, 1947)

Articled Clerk,Duffy, Tierney & Co., Auditors and Accountants, Galway, 1944-47

Temporary Accounts Clerk, Galway Corporation, 1947-48

Senior Audit Assistant, Gardner, Donnelly & Co., Dublin, 1949-50

Accountant, Dundalk UDC, 1950-55
Chief Clerk, St Conal's Hospital, Letterkenny, 1955-57
County Accountant, Meath County Council, 1957-59
Town Clerk, Drogheda Corporation, 1959-61
County Secretary, Carlow County Council, 1961-67

Waterford City Manager,1967-72
Cavan County Manager, 1972-87

Council member, AnCO (now FÁS), 1967-77
Director, An Foras Forbartha, 1979-81
Member, Executive Committee, Institute of Public Administration, 1982-86
Chairman, County and City Managers' Association, 1984-86
Member, Executive Committee, The National Road Safety Association, 1984-86
Member, Industrial Development Authority North East Region Small Industries Board, 1985-86

COLLINS, Thomas F. (1930-)

Born Galway city

BE (UCG, 1951)
MIMunE (1969)

Site Engineer, Messrs T. O'Sullivan, Contractors, Killarney, 1951-53

Temporary Engineer, Tipperary, UDC, 1953-54
Temporary Engineer, Tipperary (SR) County Council,
1954-58

Engineer, Grade III, Office of Public Works, 1958

Assistant County Engineer, Tipperary (SR) County Council, 1958-60
Assistant City Engineer, Waterford Corporation, 1960-62
Assistant County Engineer, Roscommon County Council, 1962-66
Chief Assistant County Engineer, Longford County Council, 1966-71
County Engineer, Longford County Council, 1971-74

Kerry County Manager, 1974-

Member, Industrial Development Authority South West Region Small
Industries Board, 1985-

CONLON, Michael N. (1926-)

Born County Westmeath

ACCS (1954)

Clerical Officer, Westmeath County Council, 1946-49
Town Clerk, Cavan UDC, 1949-52
Staff Officer, Louth County Council, 1952-54
Town Clerk, Ennis UCD, 1954-56
Town Clerk, Athlone UDC, 1956-57
(Seconded as Organisation and Methods Officer for Counties Longford,
Westmeath, Laois, and Offaly, 1957)
County Secretary, Tipperary (SR) County Council, 1957-58
Cork Assistant County Manager, 1959-60

Cork County Manager, 1960-78
(Seconded to Pigs and Bacon Commission as General Manager, 1963-64)

Director and Chairman, Southern Region Rehabilitation Board, 1972-
Chairman, Food, Drink and Tobacco Training Committee — FAS, 1974-
Chairman, County and City Managers' Association, 1977-78

Chief Executive, Cork and Limerick (previously Cork) Trustee Savings
Bank, 1979-90

Member, Governing Body, University College, Cork, 1968-71
Irish Representative, International Savings Banks Institute, Geneva, 1979-
Non-Executive Director, Trinity Bank Ltd, 1980-
Director, Irish American Partnership, 1982-
Chairman, Alexander Stenhouse Ltd, 1985
Member and Trustee, Cork Prison Probation Hostel, 1986-
Member, Executive Committee, Financial Services Industry
Association, 1987-
Non-Executive Director, Trading House Investment Co. Ltd, 1988-
Non-Executive Director, Bowmaker Bank Ltd, 1988-90
Fellow, Bankers' Institute of Ireland, 1989
Chairman, Bord Gais Eireann, 1990-
Vice-Chairman, European Savings Banks Group, Brussels, 1990-
Member, National Economic and Social Council, 1990-
Chairman, Mercy Hospital Board, Cork, 1990-

CONNOLLY, Donal (1942-)

Born County Waterford

ACIS (1968)
DPA (IPA,1971)

Clerical Officer, Coras Iompair Eireann, 1961-62
Clerical Officer, Cork County Council, 1962-63
Clerical Officer, Waterford County Council, 1963-69
Staff Officer, Tipperary (NR) County Council, 1969-70
Staff Officer, Waterford County Council, 1970-72
County Accountant, Tipperary (SR) County Council, 1972-77
County Secretary, Westmeath County Council, 1977-80
Tipperary (SR) Assistant County Manager, 1980-85

Roscommon County Manager, 1985-

Member, Industrial Development Authority Midlands
Region Small Industries Board, 1987-89
Chairman, Local Government Computer Services Board, 1988-89

de BUITLÉIR, Pádraig (1905-69)

Born County Tipperary

ACIS (1942)
FCIS (1963)

Clerk, Great Southern Railways (GSR), Cork, 1924-25
Accounts Clerk, Skibbereen Station, GSR, 1925-32
General Relief Clerk, GSR, 1933-34
Clerk-in-Charge, Booking Office and Parcels Department, GSR,
Kilkenny, 1934-36
Accounts Clerk, Kingsbridge Station Passenger Department, GSR, 1936
Traffic Manager's Office, Kingsbridge Station, GSR, 1936-38

Rate Inspector, Waterford County Council, 1938-44
Staff Officer, Dublin Board of Assistance, 1944
County Accountant, Carlow County Council, 1944-46
County Secretary, Tipperary (SR) County Council, 1946-56
(Temporary Tipperary (NR and SR) Assistant County Manager, 1948-56)
Tipperary (NR and SR) Assistant County Manager, 1956-64

Tipperary (NR and SR) County Manager, 1964-69
Tipperary (SR) County Manager, 1969

Volunteer, Local Defence Force, 1940-46

DEIGAN, Michael (1931-)

Born Kilkenny city

AMICEI (1956)
AMIMunE (1962)
MSc (Edinburgh, 1968)
FIEI (1971)
FIMunE (1971)
MICE (London, 1973)
FICE (London, 1984)

Trainee Engineer and Assistant Engineer (intermittently), Mahon &
McPhillips Ltd, Kilkenny, 1948-53

Clerk of Works, Carrick-on-Suir UDC, 1951-52
Clerk of Works, Nenagh UDC, 1952-53
Clerk of Works and Assistant County Engineer, Tipperary (NR) County
Council, 1953-60

Manager, Bunratty Quarry, Roadstone Ltd, 1960-62

Temporary Assistant County Engineer, Tipperary(NR) County Council, 1962-63
Assistant County Engineer, Limerick County Council, 1963-64
Assistant County Engineer, Tipperary (NR) County Council, 1964-65
Chief Assistant County Engineer, Laois County Council, 1965-74
Chief Assistant County Engineer, Tipperary (NR) County Council, 1974-75
Senior Engineer, Dublin County Council, 1975-77

Programme Manager, Mid-Western Health Board, 1977-78

Roscommon County Manager, 1978-83
Laois County Manager 1983-

Chairman, Water Pollution Advisory Council, 1980-87
Member, Construction Industry Training Committee, FAS, 1982-
Member, Industrial Development Authority Midlands Region Small Industries Board, 1985-87, 1989-

DILLON, Michael N. (1936-)

Born Cork city

Diploma in Commerce (NUI, 1958)
ACCS (1959)
Diploma in Local Administration (Gold Medal, IPA, 1967)
FCIS (1970)

Clerical Officer, Cork County Council, 1955-61
Assistant Staff Officer, Cork County Council, 1961-63
Staff Officer, Galway County Council, 1963-67
County Accountant, Limerick County Council, 1967-71
County Secretary, Limerick County Council, 1971-76

Wexford County Manager, 1976-

Member, Environment Council, 1978-81
Member, Steering Group for Irish in Local Service, 1980
Member, Fire Prevention Council, 1982-84
Member, Environment Awareness Bureau, 1985-88
Chairman, Wexford Heritage Trust Ltd, 1986-
Trustee, County Wexford Youth Trust, 1986-

Member, Irish National Committee, European Year of the Environment, 1987
Member, Industrial Development Authority South East
Region Small Industries Board, 1987-89
Deputy Chairman, Fire Services Council, 1987-
Director, National Building Agency Ltd, 1987-

DONNELLY, Patrick J. (1938-)

Born County Louth

Clerical Officer, Department of Finance, 1956-58
Executive Officer, Department of Local Government, 1959-60
Assistant Private Secretary to the Minister, Department of Local Government, 1960-64
Private Secretary to the Secretary, Department of Local Government, 1964-65
Higher Executive Officer, Department of Local Government, 1965-67
Private Secretary to the Minister, Department of Local Government, 1967-69
Assistant Principal Officer, Department of Local Government, 1969-73

County Secretary, Meath County Council, 1973-76

Kilkenny County Manager, 1976-

Chairman, South-East Regional Water Laboratory, 1979-
Member, Board of the National Safety Council, 1987-
Chairman, Kilkenny Civic Trust, 1988-
Chairman, National Authority for Occupational Health and Safety, 1989-
Member, Industrial Development Authority South East
Region Small Industries Board, 1989-
Member, Advisory Expert Committee on Local Government
Re-organisation and Reform, 1990

DONOVAN, Denis F. (1915-)

Born Cork city

ACCA (1940)
Diploma of the School of Accountancy (Glasgow, 1940)

Clerical Officer, Electricity Supply Board, 1932-40

Defence Forces, 1940-46

County Accountant, Tipperary (SR) County Council, 1946-52
(Temporary County Secretary, Tipperary (SR) County Council,
1948-52)
County Secretary, Limerick County Council, 1953-63
Assistant Manager, Cork Health Authority, 1963-66

Kilkenny County Manager, 1966-75

Management consultant in private practice, Limerick city, 1975-85

DOODY, Michael J. (1930-   )

Born Waterford city

ACCA (1963)

Clerical Officer, Waterford Corporation, 1948-56
Staff Officer, Waterford Corporation, 1956-62
Finance Officer, Waterford Corporation, 1962-75
(Temporary Waterford City Manager, 1972-75)

Waterford City Manager, 1975-

Chairman, Local Government Staff Negotiations Board, 1979-81
Chairman, Waterford Airport Ltd, 1981-90
Director, South Eastern Airport Co. Ltd, 1981-
Secretary, Garter Lane Arts Centre, 1983
Member, Industrial Development Authority South East
Region Small Industries Board, 1985-87
Member, National Archives Advisory Council, 1987-
Chairman, Local Government Computer Services Board, 1987-88
Director, Waterford Economic Development Board, 1988
Member, Helios (the European Community community action
programme for disabled people) Project Committee, 1989-
Director, Waterford Regional Airport, plc, 1990-

DOWD, Patrick (1927-   )

Born County Cavan

ACCS (1949)
DLA (IPA, 1963)
Member and Fellow of Society of Commercial Accountants (1954)
ACIS (1970)

Clerical Officer, Cavan County Council, 1946-51
Town Clerk, Clones UDC, 1951-52
Staff Officer, Louth County Council, 1952-59
Town Clerk, Ennis UDC, 1959
County Accountant, Donegal County Council, 1959-61
Town Clerk, Drogheda Corporation, 1961-64
County Secretary, Tipperary (SR) County Council, 1964-67

Laois-Offaly County Manager, 1968-81
Cork County Manager, 1981-

Chairman, County and City Managers' Association, 1978-79
Chairman, Local Government Computer Services Board, 1986-87
Member, Industrial Development Authority South West Region Small
Industries Board, 1985-
Member, National Roads Authority, 1988-

DOYLE, Patrick J. (1931-)

Born County Galway

DLA (IPA, 1965)

Clerical Officer, Westmeath County Council, 1951-60
Town Clerk, Buncrana UDC, 1960
Staff Officer, Donegal County Council, 1960-63
Town Clerk, Dungarvan UDC, 1963-67
County Accountant, Mayo County Council, 1967-71
(Director, Galway/Mayo Regional Development Group, 1970-71)
County Secretary, Sligo County Council, 1971-76
Cork Assistant County Manager, 1976-78

Leitrim County Manager, 1978-

Member, Industrial Development Authority Donegal and
North West Regions Small Industries Board, 1985-

EGAN, Michael J. (1875-1944)

Born County Mayo

Apprentice, Grocery and Hardware, Mr E. Carney, Castlebar, 1890-94
Employee, Grocery and Hardware, Mr C.M. Church, Carrick-on-
Shannon, 1894-98

71

Employee, Grocery and Hardware, Mr P.J. Joyce, Longford, 1898-1902
In grocery and hardware business on own account, 1903-08

Clerk, Mayo County Council, 1908-14
County Accountant, Mayo County Council, 1914-19
County Secretary, Mayo County Council, 1919-42

County Commissioner, Mayo, 1940-42

Mayo County Manager, 1942-44

Member, Commission of Inquiry into De-rating, 1929-31

Secretary, for a period, Castlebar Branch, United Irish League
Secretary, for a period, Castlebar Town Tenants' League
In 1920 Mr Egan was arrested and courtmartialled for refusing to
disclose to the Local Government Board the name of the Treasurer of
Mayo County Council.

Note: The United Irish League was founded at Westport on 23 January
1898 by William O'Brien MP (who was at that time residing at nearby
Clew Bay) to organise agitation aimed at dividing up grazing lands
among small farmers. The first branch was established at Westport on
6 February 1898. Through the influence of the League, unity was
re-established within the Irish Party on 30 January 1900 after nine years
of the 'split'.

FEELY, Francis J. (1931-)

Born Dublin city

ACCA (1956)

Clerical Officer, Dublin Corporation, 1949-55
Class A Officer, Dublin Corporation, 1955-60
Minor Staff Officer, Dublin Corporation, 1960
Organisation and Methods Officer, Dublin Corporation, 1960-61
Assistant Principal Officer, Dublin Corporation, 1962-66
Principal Officer, Dublin Corporation, 1966-69
Dublin Assistant City and County Manager, 1969-79
(Housing Co-ordinator, Dublin City and County, 1976-79)

72

Dublin City and County Manager, 1979-

President, Institute of Public Administration, 1986-

FLANNERY, Michael (1908-)

Born County Clare

BComm (UCD, 1934)
BA (TCD, 1936)
MA (TCD, 1963)

Clerical Officer, Department of Local Government and Public Health, 1926-35

County Accountant, Cavan County Council, 1935-39
Town Clerk, An Uaimh UDC, 1939-40
Borough Accountant, Dun Laoghaire Corporation, 1940-44
County Secretary, Cork County Council, 1944-45

Wicklow County Manager, 1945-73

Director, National Mass-Radiography Association, 1951-58
Member, Blood Transfusion Service Board, 1958-66
Member, Consultative Committees (Planning and Development; Nature and Amenity Conservation and Development), An Foras Forbartha, 1964-72

Part-time Lecturer, School of Commerce and Public Organisation, Trinity College, Dublin, 1959-63
Visiting Lecturer, University of Birmingham, 1968, 1969

Academic Adviser (Institute of Public Administration Diplomas), 1973-79
Part-time Lecturer, Institute of Public Administration, 1974-83

Author, *Sanitation, Conservation and Recreation Services in Ireland*, IPA, Dublin, 1976
Author, *A History of Greystones Rugby Football Club*, Greystones Rugby Football Club, 1978
Author, *Building Land Prices*, The Tribune Printing and Publishing Group, Birr, 1980

73

FLYNN, John P. (1898-1974)

Born County Tipperary

B Comm (UCC,1919)

Accounts Department, Dwyer & Co. Ltd, Cork, 1919-20
Book-keeping and Foreign Exchange, Anglo-South American Bank
Ltd, London, 1920
General Banking, Discounts and Foreign Exchange, Anglo-South
American Bank Ltd, Rosario de Santa Fe, Argentina, 1920-25

County Accountant, Limerick County Council, 1926-28

Accountant, The Agricultural Credit Corporation, Dublin, 1928-30

County Secretary, Tipperary (NR) County Council, 1930-42

Tipperary (NR and SR) County Manager, 1942-63

Temporary Tipperary (NR and SR) County Manager, 1963-64

Gave series of lectures on Local Government Administration, UCD,
1940-42

Member, National Health Council, 1958-64
Chairman, County and City Managers' Association, 1960-63

Governor, St Laurence's Hospital, Dublin, for a period following his
retirement

GAVIN, Joseph O. (1935-)

Born County Westmeath

B Comm (UCD, 1962)

Substitute Teacher, Moate, County Westmeath, 1954-55
Underwriting Clerk, Motor Section, Insurance Corporation of Ireland,
1955-56

Clerical Officer, Kildare County Council, 1957-63
Town Clerk, Carrickmacross UDC, 1963-64
Staff Officer, Offaly County Council, 1964-67
County Accountant, Wicklow County Council, 1967-72

County Secretary, Westmeath County Council, 1973-76
Clare Assistant County Manager, 1976-77

Monaghan County Manager, 1977-

Member, Industrial Development Authority North East
Region Small Industries Board, 1986-89

Region Small Industries Board, 1986-89

County Secretary, Westmeath County Council, 1973-76
Clare Assistant County Manager, 1976-77

Monaghan County Manager, 1977-

HASLAM, Richard B. (1925-   )

Born County Cork

BComm (UCC, 1951)

Clerical Officer, Cork County Council, 1946-54
Assistant Staff Officer, Cork County Council, 1954
Town Clerk, Youghal UDC, 1954-58
City Accountant, Cork Corporation, 1958-63
(Seconded to Cork Health Authority as temporary
Secretary/Accountant, 1960-63)
County Secretary, Limerick County Council, 1963-66
Cork Assistant County Manager, 1966-70
(Seconded to Limerick County Council as Deputy County Manager,
1967-68)

Limerick County Manager, 1970-88

Member, Muintir na Tíre Review Committee, 1974
Member, Combat Poverty Advisory Committee, 1974-76
Director, Rent-an-Irish Cottage Ltd, 1976-78
Chairman, County and City Managers' Association, 1979-80
Member, Public Service Advisory Council, 1979-83
Member, Legal Aid Board, 1979-85
Member, Aughinish Alumina Review Committee, 1980
Director, National Building Agency Ltd, 1983-86
Member, Cospoir, 1985-88

Part-time Assistant, UCC, 1955-62
Part-time Lecturer, UCC, 1962-72
Lecturer, Department of Public Administration, UCC, 1973-88
Adjunct Associate Professor, NIHE (now University of Limerick), 1984-

Head, Department of Public Administration, UCC, 1988-

Member, Adult Education Committee, UCC, 1972-
Member, Governing Body, Mary Immaculate Training College,
Limerick, 1977-
Member, Governing Body, NIHE (now University of Limerick), 1982-
Member, Board of Business and Humanities, National Council for
Educational Awards, 1985-
Trustee, Mary Immaculate Training College, Limerick, 1986-

Member, Advisory Expert Committee on Local Government
Re-organisation and Reform, 1990

HAYES, Robert N. (1926-)

Born Cork city

BE (UCD, 1948)
MSc (Ohio State University, 1964)
FIEI (1970)
FIMunE (1970)
FICE (1977)
FCIT (1977)

Junior Engineer, Nicholas O'Dwyer, Consulting Engineer, Dublin,
1948-49

Temporary Resident Engineer, Design Engineer and Assistant County
Engineer, Dublin County Council, 1949-52
Temporary Engineer, Grade II, Dublin Corporation, 1952-54
Engineer, Grade II, Dublin Corporation, 1954-61
(Temporary Grade I Engineer, Dublin Corporation, 1954-59)

Engineering Inspector (Roads), Department of Local Government,
1961-65
(Fellowship from International Roads Federation to study in USA,
1963-64)
Research Officer (Traffic Engineering), An Foras Forbartha, 1965-67

Senior Engineer, BKS Technical Services, 1967
Partner, McCarthy and Partners, Consulting Engineers, 1967-68

County Engineer, Cavan County Council, 1968-70

Tipperary (SR) County Manager, 1970-75

Member, Public Service Advisory Council, 1971-74

General Manager, Dublin Port and Docks Board, 1975-90

Council Member, Institute of Transport in Ireland, 1977-81
Council Member, Institution of Engineers of Ireland, 1979-86
Chairman, Institute of Transport in Ireland, 1980-81
President, Institution of Engineers of Ireland, 1985-86

Chairman, An Post Pension Trust, 1990-
Director, Oppenheim International Finance Bank, 1990-

Executive Director, McCarthy and Partners, Consulting
Engineers, 1990-

HAYES, Seamus (1930-)

Born County Tipperary

Associate of the Corporation of Secretaries (1961)

Clerical Officer, Tipperary (SR) County Council, 1948-57
Staff Officer, Tipperary (SR) County Council, 1957-67
County Accountant, Tipperary (SR) County Council, 1967-71
County Secretary, Longford County Council, 1971-74
Kerry Assistant County Manager, 1974-77

Wicklow County Manager, 1977-84
Tipperary (SR) County Manager, 1984-

Member, Industrial Development Authority South East
Region Small Industries Board, 1985-87
Chairman, Local Government Computer Services Board, 1989-

77

HAYES, Thomas A. (1907-65)

Born County Cork

Town Clerk, Skibbereen UDC, 1929-34
Town Clerk and Secretary, Gas Department, Mallow UDC, 1934-38
Town Clerk, Dundalk UDC, 1938-40
County Secretary, Westmeath County Council, 1940-42

County Commissioner, Westmeath, 1940-42

Longford-Westmeath County Manager, 1942-43

Tipperary (NR and SR) Assistant County Manager, 1944-45
Cork Assistant County Manager, 1945-65
(Seconded to Kerry County Council as Deputy County Manager, 1949)

HEALY, Patrick T. (1880-1948)

Born County Wicklow

Shorthand-Clerk, Royal Dublin Society, Kildare Street, 1897-98
Clerk, Messrs Richard Dickeson & Sons Ltd, Army Contractors, Upper
Exchange Street, Dublin, 1898-99

Junior Clerk, Wicklow County Council, 1899, with various promotions
to 1914
Chief Clerk, Wicklow County Council, 1914-22
Part-time teacher of commercial subjects for thirteen years in
Wicklow and for two years in Arklow under the County Wicklow Joint
Technical Instruction Committee
Clerk, County Wicklow Old Age Pensions Committee, 1922-42
County Secretary, Wicklow County Council, 1922-42

County Commissioner, Wicklow, 1940-42

Wicklow County Manager, 1942-45

HEGARTY, Denis A. (1907-)

Born Cork city

BA, BComm (UCC, 1930)

General Secretary, Irish Local Government Officials' Union, 1931-32

Borough Accountant, Dun Laoghaire Corporation, 1933-40
County Secretary, Westmeath County Council, 1940

County Commissioner, Westmeath, 1940

Waterford City Manager, 1940-43
Leitrim-Sligo County Manager, 1943-46

General Manager, Dublin Port and Docks Board, 1946-74

HERNON, Patrick J. (1889-1973)

Born Galway city

B Comm (UCG, 1919)
Research Scholarship, London School of Economics
(London University, 1919-21)
LLD (honoris causa) (NUI, 1943)

Inspector, Local Government Department, Dáil Éireann, 1921-23
Commissioner, Cork Poor Law Union, 1923-24
Commissioner (one of three), Dublin Corporation, 1924-30
Commissioner, Dublin Board of Guardians, 1929-30
Dun Laoghaire Borough Manager, 1930-37

Dublin City Manager, 1937-42
Dublin City and County Manager, 1942-55
(Appointed County Manager by Section 4 (7) (a) of the County
Management Act, 1940)

Note: Dublin County Council was dissolved on 26 September 1941 and
Daniel J.O' Donovan (later Proinsias MacBearnaird) was appointed
Commissioner. By virtue of Section 7 (1) of the County Management
(Amendment) Act 1942, the Commissioner exercised the executive
functions of Dublin County Council (from 26 August 1942) for the
duration of the dissolution of the Council (until 1948). During that
period, the Dublin County Manager exercised the executive functions of
Dun Laoghaire Corporation and Balbriggan Town Commissioners only.

HIGGINS, John J. (1936-)

Born County Cork

Diploma in Administration (IPA, 1966)

Clerical Officer, Cork County Council, 1955-65
Staff Officer, Clare County Council, 1965-72

County Accountant, Waterford County Council, 1972-74
County Secretary, Wicklow County Council, 1974-77
Assistant City Manager, Cork Corporation, 1977-87

Limerick City Manager, 1987-

HURLEY, Daniel (1931-)

Born Cork city

Diploma in Commerce (UCC, 1955)
Member of the Corporation of Secretaries (1958)
Associate Member of the Institute of Personnel Management (1971)

Clerical Officer, Land Commission, 1949-50

Clerical Officer, Cork Corporation, 1950-64
Staff Officer, Cork Corporation, 1964-66
Staff Personnel Officer, Cork Corporation, 1966-69

Industrial Relations Officer, Irish Dunlop Company Ltd, 1969-71

Personnel Officer, Southern Health Board, 1971-75
Programme Manager, Mid-Western Health Board, 1975-76

Cork Assistant County Manager, 1976-77

Westmeath County Manager, 1978-80
Waterford County Manager, 1980-

Director, Tramore Failte Ltd, 1981-
Chairman, Local Government Computer Services Board, 1982-84
Director, Housing Finance Agency plc, 1982-
Chairman, Dungarvan Tourism Ltd, 1983-90
Director, Waterford Airport plc, 1985-
Member, Industrial Development Authority South East
Region Small Industries Board, 1987-89
Director, Tramore Properties Developments Ltd, 1989-

HURLEY, James (1902-65)

Born County Cork

BComm, (UCC, 1932)
BA (UCC, 1940)

Town Clerk, Clonakilty UDC, 1924-33
County Accountant, Meath County Council, 1933-35
County Secretary, Longford County Council, 1935-37

Commissioner, Longford UDC, 1935-37
Secretary, South Cork Board of Health and Secretary, South Cork
Board of Assistance, 1937-42
Commissioner, Passage West UDC, 1938-42

Meath County Manager, 1942-43

Cork Assistant County Manager, 1943-44

Secretary and Bursar, University College, Cork, 1944-65

JOHNSTON, Brian (1942-)

Born County Cavan

Certificate in Public Administration (IPA, 1972)
Certificate in Management (IMI, 1974)

Clerk, Córas Iompair Éireann, 1960-62

Clerical Officer, Cavan County Council, 1962-67
Town Clerk, Westport UDC, 1967-68
Staff Officer, Longford County Council, 1968-70
County Development Officer, Longford County Development Team,
1970-72
County Development Officer, Louth County Council, 1972-76
Town Clerk, Dundalk UDC, 1976-78
County Secretary, Wicklow County Council, 1978-85
Wicklow Assistant County Manager, 1985-89

Cavan County Manager, 1989-

Director, National Development Corporation Ltd, 1986-
Director, Cavan County Enterprise Fund Ltd, 1988-

JOYCE, Edmond A. (1894-1950)

Born County Kilkenny

AIAA (1927)

Junior and Ledger Clerk, Irish Agricultural Organisation Society, 1911-19
Inspection and Audit Department, Irish Agricultural Organisation
Society, 1919-28

81

County Accountant, Galway County Council, 1928-31
County Secretary, Louth County Council, 1931-42

County Commissioner, Louth, 1940-42

Carlow-Kildare County Manager, 1942-44
Louth County Manager, 1944-50

First Honorary Secretary and Treasurer, County and City Managers'
Association, 1943-47

KEATING, Seamus (1930-)

Born County Tipperary

Clerical Officer, Tipperary (SR) County Council, 1948-57
Staff Officer and Rate Collector, Waterford County Council, 1957-63
County Accountant, Tipperary (SR) County Council, 1963-66
County Secretary, Donegal County Council, 1966-70

Kerry County Manager, 1970-73
Galway County Manager, 1973-85
Galway City and County Manager, 1986-
(Became City Manager by virtue of Section 7 (6) of the Local
Government (Re-organisation) Act 1985)

Member, UCG Board of Extra Mural Studies, 1975-
Chairman, County and City Managers' Association, 1980-82
Member, Travelling People Review Body, 1981-83
Chairman, Local Government Computer Services Board, 1984-85
Member, Industrial Development Authority West Region Small
Industries Board, 1985-
Chairman, Local Government Staff Negotiations Board, 1987-89
Director, Galway Boston Ventures Ltd, 1987-

KILLEEN, Michael J. (1940-)

Born Limerick city

DPA (IPA, 1966)
Associate Member of the Chartered Institute of Secretaries (1966)

Temporary Library Assistant, Limerick Corporation, 1959
Clerical Officer, Limerick Corporation, 1959-60

82

Clerical Officer, Limerick Health Authority, 1960-63
Town Clerk, Trim UDC, 1963
Clerical Officer, Limerick Health Authority, 1963-64
Town Clerk, Cashel UDC, 1964-66
Town Clerk, Nenagh UDC, 1966-68
Town Clerk, Tullamore UDC, 1968-69
County Accountant, Laois County Council, 1969-71

Finance Officer, Midland Health Board, 1971-74
Programme Manager, Western Health Board, 1974-77

Longford County Manager, 1978-

Member, Transport Consultative Commission, 1983-84
Member, Industrial Development Authority Midlands
Region Small Industries Board, 1985-87, 1989-
Member, Health Promotion Advisory Council, 1988-

LAVIN, Patrick (1925-)

Born County Roscommon

Diploma in Local Administration (IPA, 1964)

Temporary Clerical Officer, Roscommon County Council, 1946-52
Town Clerk, Letterkenny UDC, 1952-56
Town Clerk, Enniscorthy UDC, 1956-65
Town Clerk, Athlone UDC, 1965-66
Town Clerk, Dundalk UDC, 1966-69
County Secretary, Louth County Council, 1969-74
Cork Assistant County Manager, 1974-75

Monaghan County Manager, 1975-77
Louth County Manager, 1977-87

Member, Council of Institute of Public Administration, 1972-85
Member, Council of Co-Operation North, 1979-
Member, Industrial Development Authority North East Region
Small Industries Board, 1985-87

LAWLOR, Dermot C. (1905-87)

Born County Dublin

BComm (UCD, 1925)

Clerk, Accounts Department, Browne & Nolan Ltd, Dublin, 1926-29
Articled Clerk, Patrick Butler, Chartered Accountant, Dublin, 1929-32

Senior Assistant, Patrick Butler, Chartered Accountant, Dublin, 1932-34

Accountant and Assistant Secretary, Hospitals' Commission, 1934
Accountant, Turf Development Board Ltd, 1934-36
Chief Administrative Officer, Turf Development Board Ltd, 1936-37
Secretary, Turf Development Board Ltd, 1937-44

Meath County Manager, 1944-47

General Manager, Bord na Mona, 1947-58
Managing Director, Bord na Mona, 1958-73

McCARTHY, Dermot M. (1906-83)

Born Dublin city

ACIS
FFCS (1937)
AIIS

Clerk, Great Southern Railways, Dublin, 1923-29
Clerk, Cahill & Co. Ltd, Dublin, 1929-34
Manager, Bailey, Son & Gibson Ltd, Dublin, 1934-38
Assistant Manager, Cahill & Co. Ltd, Dublin, 1938-40
Works Manager, The Irish Times, 1940-41

Town Clerk, Enniscorthy UDC, 1941-44
County Secretary, Monaghan County Council, 1945-46

Cavan County Manager, 1946-71

Temporary Cavan County Manager, 1971-72

Honorary Secretary, County and City Managers' Association, 1957-63

MacCARTHY, Seán P. (1933-)

Born County Cork

BE (UCC, 1954)
AMICEI (1959)
MI Mun E (1963)
C Eng MIEI (1969)
MICE (1971)

84

Contractor's Engineer, Edward Barrett & Sons, Ballintemple, Cork, 1954-58

Temporary Engineer, Cork County Council, 1958-60
Temporary Assistant County Engineer, Cork County Council, 1960-62
Temporary Assistant City Engineer, Cork Corporation, 1962
Temporary Assistant County Engineer, Laois County Council, 1962-63
Assistant County Engineer (Design), Tipperary (NR) County Council, 1963-67
Chief Assistant County Engineer, Waterford County Council, 1967-75
County Engineer, Offaly County Council, 1975-82

Donegal County Manager, 1982
Offaly County Manager, 1982-

Member, Industrial Development Authority Midlands Region
Small Industries Board, 1987-89

MacDIARMADA, Tomás P. (1917-82)

Born Cork city

BA (UCC, 1938)
B Comm (UCC, 1938)
ASAA (1941)
AICAI (1957)

Articled Clerk, C.P. McCarthy, Accountant and Auditor, Cork, 1938-42

Accounts Clerk, Galway Corporation, 1942-43
Staff Officer, Monaghan County Council, 1943-46
County Accountant, Dublin County Council, 1946-48
County Secretary, Wexford County Council, 1948-57
Galway Assistant County Manager, 1957-59

Limerick City Manager, 1959-82

Chairman, Local Government Staff Negotiations Board, 1973-74
and 1975-76
Chairman, County and City Managers' Association, 1975-76
Chairman, Local Government Computer Services Board, 1978-81

MacEVILLY, Walter (1920-)

Born County Mayo

ACIS (1947)
DPA (UCD, 1949)
FCIS (1952)
Solicitor (1979)

Clerical Officer, Mayo County Council, 1938-47
Staff Officer, Dublin Board of Assistance, 1947-49
Secretary, South Cork Board of Public Assistance, 1949-52
County Secretary, Laois County Council, 1952-54

Clare County Manager, 1954-59
Cork City Manager, 1959-70

Chief Executive Officer, Southern Health Board, 1970-78

Director, National Mass-radiography Association, 1950-58
Member, National Health Council, 1972-78
Chairman, Local Government Staff Negotiations Board, 1974-75

In practice as solicitor in Cork city, 1979-

Chairman, Travelling People Review Body, 1981-83

McGEENEY, Michael G. (1906-83)

Born County Armagh

Corporation of Accountants (Robert Gardner Gold Medallist in
Accountancy subjects, 1931)

Junior Executive Officer, Revenue Commissioners, 1925-31
Local Government Auditor, Department of Local Government and
Public Health, 1932-44
(Seconded as temporary Waterford City Manager, 1943-44)

Longford-Westmeath County Manager, 1944-69

86

McGEOUGH, Peter (1881-1948)

Born County Monaghan

Assistant Clerk, Monaghan County Council, 1900-06
Secretary, Monaghan Committee of Agriculture and Secretary, County
Monaghan Joint Committee of Technical Instruction, 1906-25
Part-time clerk, Monaghan UDC, 1910-25
Secretary, Monaghan County Council, 1925-42
Commissioner, Monaghan Board of Health and Public Assistance,
1940-42

County Commissioner, Monaghan, 1940-42

Monaghan County Manager, 1942-47

McGINLEY, John (1934-)

Born County Meath

ACIS (1960)
DLA (IPA, 1963)
Diploma in Social Studies, International Foundation for Adult Studies,
The Netherlands (1990)

Grade III Clerk, An Bord Iascaigh Mhara, 1952-59
District Court Clerk, Grade VII, Department of Justice, 1959-60

Town Clerk, Cavan UDC, 1960-62
Borough Accountant, Sligo Corporation, 1962-65
Town Clerk, Ballina UDC, 1965-70
Town Clerk, Drogheda Corporation, 1970-75
County Secretary, Clare County Council, 1975-78

Tipperary (NR) County Manager, 1978-

Director, Rent-an-Irish Cottage Ltd, 1979-84
Member, Building and Grants Committee, Shannon Free Airport
Development Company (SFADCo), 1980-87
Member, Irish Water Safety Association, 1983-87
Member, Council of State Agencies Development Cooperation
Organisation (DEVCO), 1989-

Commandant, Forsa Cosanta Áitiúil, 1980-

McHUGH, Thomas J. (1926-   )

Born Galway city

Temporary Clerical Officer, Limerick Corporation, 1946-48
Clerical Officer, Limerick Corporation, 1948-53
Staff Officer, Limerick Corporation, 1953
Assistant Town Clerk, Limerick Corporation, 1953-71
(Director, Limerick, Clare and Tipperary (NR) Regional Development
Organisation, 1968-71)
County Secretary, Tipperary (SR) County Council, 1971-74

Cork City Manager, 1974-86

Member, Industrial Development Authority South West
Region Small Industries Board, 1985-86

General Manager, Bord Gais Eireann, Southern Region, 1986-90

Director, First National Building Society, 1986-
Director, Triskel Arts Centre, Cork, 1986-
Trustee, Irish National Ballet Trust Fund, 1988-
Director, Cork Media Communications Ltd, Cork, 1989-
Director, National Sculpture Factory, Cork, 1989-

MacKELL, James L. (1911-80)

Born Dublin city

ACCA (1934)
ACIS (1941)
FCIS (1945)

Irish Shell Ltd, Fleet Street, Dublin, 1928-36
Industrial Alcohol Distributors' Association, Dublin, 1936-44
Member, Petrol Distributors' Committee, Dublin, 1939-44

County Secretary, Louth County Council, 1944-52
(Temporary Louth County Manager, 1950-52)

Louth County Manager, 1952-76

Director, Eastern Regional Tourism Organisation Ltd, 1965-67
Chairman, County and City Managers' Association, 1966-69
Member, Blood Transfusion Service Board, 1967-72

MACKEN, Matthew (1911-)

Born County Galway

BA, BComm (UCG, 1933)

Chief Ledger Clerk, Comhlucht Siúicre Éireann Teo, Tuam, 1934-38

Chief Clerk, Joint Mental Hospital Board, Ballinasloe, 1938-44
County Secretary, Galway County Council, 1944-46

Limerick City Manager, 1946-59
Carlow-Kildare County Manager, 1959-65
Dublin City and County Manager, 1965-76

Founder Director, National Mass-radiography Association, 1950-55
Member, Special Advisory Committee on Over-Crowding in Mental
Hospitals, 1955
Member, National Health Council, 1958-71
Member, Commission on Itinerancy, 1960-63
Member, Commission of Inquiry on Mental Illness, 1961-66
Chairman, County and City Managers' Association, 1964-66

Governor, Irish Times Trust, 1976-
Director, Irish Times Ltd, 1976-
Administrative Adviser to The Royal Dublin Society, 1976-81
Director, Ballsbridge Sales Ltd, 1978-85
Director, Ballsbridge Tattersalls Ltd, 1979-85
Director, First National Building Society, 1976-86
Chairman, First National Building Society, 1979-80 and 1984-85

MACKEY, David (1949-)

Born County Donegal

Certificate in Public Administration (IPA, 1972)
Certificate in Public Sector Economics (IPA, 1989)

Clerical Officer, Donegal County Council, 1967-73
Town Clerk, Kinsale UDC, 1973
Town Clerk, Letterkenny UDC, 1973-74
Staff Officer, Donegal County Council, 1974-75
Administrative Officer, Donegal County Council, 1975-81
County Secretary, Tipperary (SR) County Council, 1981-85
Tipperary (SR) Assistant County Manager, 1985-88

Cavan County Manager, 1988-89

Director, County Cavan Enterprise Committee, 1988-
Member, Management Committee, County Cavan Tourism Council, 1988-
Member, Industrial Development Authority North East Region Small Industries Board, 1989

General Manager, Sean Quinn Group, Derrylin, County Fermanagh, 1989-

MacLOCHLAINN, Liam (Liam McLoughlin) (1905-   )

Born County Kerry

BComm (UCC, 1926)

Secondary Teacher, Christian Brothers School, Lismore, County Waterford, 1927-28
Employee, Agricultural Credit Corporation, Dublin, 1928-32

Assistant Leader Writer, *Irish Press*, Dublin, 1932-33
London Editor, *Irish Press*, London, 1933-37

Accountant, Meath Board of Health and Public Assistance, 1937-38
Town Clerk, Carlow UDC, 1938-39
Secretary, Monaghan Board of Health and Public Assistance, 1939-40
Town Clerk, Secretary and Accountant to Gas Undertaking, Clonmel Corporation, 1940-42
County Secretary, Sligo County Council, 1942-44

Mayo County Manager, 1944-70

Temporary Mayo County Manager, 1970-71

MacLOCHLAINN, Seán D. (1897-1957)

Born County Louth

Employee, Hibernian Bank Ltd, 1913-24
Clerk, County Donegal Insurance Committee, 1924-30

County Secretary, Donegal County Council, 1924-42

County Commissioner, Donegal, 1940-42

Donegal County Manager, 1942-57

Acted for Ballyshannon Town Commissioners, 1942-50
(No candidate was nominated for election as Town Commissioner at the 1942 or 1945 local elections)

Commissioner, Buncrana UDC, 1952-55

Chairman, County and City Managers' Association, 1955-56

McMANUS, Thomas J. (1911-82)

Born County Meath

Law Clerk with A.J. Malone, Solicitor, Trim, County Meath, 1928-33
Law Clerk with Messrs Meehan & Co., Solicitors, Portlaoise, 1933-39

Town Clerk, Portlaoise Town Commissioners, 1937-39
Town Clerk, Carrick-on-Suir UDC, 1940-47
(Temporary County Secretary, Tipperary (SR) County Council, 1945-46)
(Temporary County Secretary, Kilkenny County Council, 1946-47)
(Temporary County Secretary, Kildare County Council, 1947)
County Secretary, Donegal County Council, 1947-59
(Seconded as temporary Leitrim-Sligo County Manager, 1958-59)

Leitrim-Sligo County Manager, 1959-76

Temporary Sligo County Manager, 1976-77

Member, National Health Council, 1964-72
Director, North-Western Regional Tourism Organisation Ltd, 1966-82

MAHON, Desmond P. (1946-)

Born County Roscommon

Diploma in Public Administration (IPA, 1969)
Certificate of School of Public Administration (IPA, 1971)

Clerical Officer, Roscommon County Council, 1964-71
Town Clerk, Skibbereen UDC, 1971

Staff Officer, Western Health Board, 1972-73
Internal Auditor, Western Health Board, 1973-77
Financial Accountant, Western Health Board, 1977-80

Finance Officer, Clare County Council, 1980-85
Donegal Assistant County Manager, 1985-90

Mayo County Manager, 1990-

Member, Industrial Development Authority West Region
Small Industries Board, 1990-

MEGHEN, Patrick J. (1901-71)

Born Dublin city

BE (UCD, 1921)
BSc, (UCD, 1921)
MICEI

Clerk, Local Government Department, Dáil Éireann, 1921-22
Engineering Inspector, Department of Local Government and Public
Health, 1922-28
Commissioner, Tipperary UDC, 1924-28
Commissioner, Ennis UDC, 1926-34*
Commissioner, Bray UDC, 1928-34
Commissioner, Howth UDC, 1928-34
Commissioner, Bundoran UDC, 1929-30
Commissioner, Wicklow UDC, 1932-34
Commissioner, Kilkenny County Council, Kilkenny Board of Health and
Public Assistance and Kilkenny Mental Hospital Committee, 1934-37

Commissioner, Waterford Corporation, 1937-39
Commissioner, Tipperary (SR) County Council and Tipperary (SR)
Board of Health and Public Assistance, 1934-42 (also administered affairs
of Fethard Town Commissioners)

County Commissioner, Tipperary (NR) and (SR), 1940-42

Limerick County Manager, 1942-61

Vice-President, Muintir na Tíre, 1945-70
Member, Commission on Emigration and other Population Problems,
1948-54
Chairman, County and City Managers' Association, 1953-54

92

Director of Studies (Institute of Public Administration Diplomas),
1961-71

Author, *Local Government: A Guide for the Citizen*, IPA, 1959
Author, *A Short History of the Public Service*, IPA, 1962
Author, *Housing in Ireland*, IPA, 1963
Author, *Statistics in Ireland*, IPA, 1963
Part-author, *The Limerick Rural Survey 1958-1964*, Muintir na Tíre, 1964
Author, *Roads in Ireland*, IPA, 1966

*His original term of office as Commissioner for Ennis UDC expired on
14 April 1929. The necessary steps were taken locally to hold an election
for a new council, but no candidate was nominated. It was the desire of
the people of Ennis that Mr Meghen should remain in charge of the
administration for a longer period, and the absence of candidates at the
election was one of the ways in which local opinion expressed itself. The
matter was, in the ordinary course, referred to the Clare County Council
that they might appoint persons to act for the Urban District Council
until a proper election was held. The County Council, however, did not
nominate any persons to carry on the administration but requested the
Minister to nominate Mr Meghen for a further term. It was not possible
to comply with this request without fresh legislation. This legislation was
embodied in the Ennis Urban District Council (Dissolution) Act 1929.

MOLLOY, James B. (1917-)

Born Dublin city

Class C Clerk, Dublin Corporation, 1935-38
Class B Clerk Dublin Corporation, 1938-46
Class A Clerk Dublin Corporation, 1946-50
Minor Staff Officer, Dublin Corporation, 1950-54
Senior Executive Officer, Dublin Corporation, 1954-55
Assistant Principal Officer, Dublin Corporation, 1955-58
Principal Officer, Dublin Corporation, 1958-66
Dublin Assistant City and County Manager, 1966-76
(Housing Co-ordinator, Dublin City and County, 1973-76)

Dublin City and County Manager, 1976-79

Member, Public Service Advisory Council, 1976-77

Member, National Executive, Irish Wheelchair Association, 1984-

MOLONEY, Francis (1934-   )

Born County Clare

Diploma in Social and Economic Science (UCG, 1956)
B Comm (UCC, 1967)

Apprentice Reporter, *Clare Champion*, 1952-53

Temporary Clerical Officer, Clare County Council, 1953-55
Clerical Officer, Clare County Council, 1955-59
Town Clerk, Youghal UDC, 1959-69
County Accountant, Wexford County Council, 1969-70
Town Clerk, Dundalk UDC, 1970-72
County Secretary, Leitrim County Council, 1972-78
Cork Assistant County Manager, 1978-83

Donegal County Manager, 1983-

Member, Industrial Development Authority Donegal and North West Regions Small Industries Board, 1985-

MONAHAN, Philip (1894-1983)

Born Dublin city

MComm (*honoris causa*) (NUI, 1949)

Secondary Teacher, Christian Brothers' School, Drogheda, 1915-23

Commissioner, Kerry County Council and Kerry County Board of Health, 1923-24
Commissioner, West Cork County Board of Health, 1924-25
Commissioner, Cobh UDC, 1924-28
Commissioner, South Cork County Board of Public Assistance, 1925-27
Commissioner, Cork District Mental Hospital Committee, 1925-28
Commissioner, Cork Corporation, 1924-29

County Commissioner, Cork, 1940-42

Cork City Manager, 1929-58
(Appointed by Section 10 (1) of the Cork City Management Act 1929)

Chairman, County and City Managers' Association, 1947-53

Mayor, Drogheda Corporation, 1920-25
Member, Louth County Council, 1920-25

For a developed profile see page 116

94

MOYNIHAN, Simon J. (1899-1966)

Born County Clare

Established Clerk to Inspector of Taxes, Cork, 1916-19
Organiser, Dáil Éireann Loan, 1919-20
Inspector, Local Government Department, Dáil Éireann, 1920-22

Accountant and Income Tax Expert, 1924-29

Junior Executive Officer, Office of Public Works, 1929-34
Inspector, Department of Local Government and Public Health, 1934

Commissioner, Waterford County Council and Waterford Board of
Health and Public Assistance, 1934-42
Commissioner, Kilkenny County Council and Kilkenny Board of Health
and Public Assistance, 1937-42
Commissioner, Kilkenny Corporation, 1942-45

County Commissioner, Kilkenny, 1940-42

Kilkenny-Waterford County Manager, 1942-64

Temporary Kilkenny-Waterford County Manager, 1964-65
Temporary Waterford County Manager, 1965-66

MURPHY, Daniel C. (1900-54)

Born County Cork

Fellow, Institute of Company Accountants (1934)

Clerk, Cashier and Accountant and Manager from 1928, Messrs. J.
O'Shea & Co., Wholesale Manufacturers and Distributors, Macroom,
1921-31

Town Clerk, Mallow UDC, and Secretary, Mallow UDC Gas Works,
1931-33
Secretary, North Cork Board of Health and Public Assistance, 1933-42

Louth County Manager, 1942-43

Cork Assistant County Manager, 1943-54

MURPHY, Patrick J. (1930-)

Born County Offaly

BE (UCG, 1951)
DPA (UCD, 1953)
FIEI (1990)
Certified Diploma in Accounting and Finance (ACCA, 1978)

Civil Engineer, Electricity Supply Board, 1951-52

Trainee Engineer and Temporary Grade II Engineer, Dublin
Corporation, 1952-57

Senior Field Engineer, Lammus Co. Ltd, Whitegate, County
Cork, 1957-58
Agent/Engineer, P. Carvill & Sons, Warrenpoint, County Down, 1959-60

Temporary Assistant County Engineer, Tipperary (NR) County Council,
1960
Assistant Borough Engineer, Dun Laoghaire Corporation, 1960-62
Engineer, Grade II, Dublin Corporation, 1962
Assistant County Engineer, Tipperary (NR) County Council, 1962-66
Chief Assistant County Engineer, Limerick County Council, 1966-76
Limerick Assistant County Manager, 1976-89
(Temporary Limerick County Manager, 1988-89)

Limerick County Manager, 1989-

MURRAY, Edward M. (1909-88)

Born Dublin city

Corporation of Registered Accountants (1937)

Clerical Officer, Dublin Corporation, 1926-29

Executive Officer, Electricity Supply Board, 1929-45

Chief Clerk, Grangegorman Mental Hospital Board, 1945-58

Laois-Offaly County Manager, 1958-66
Carlow-Kildare County Manager, 1966-74

NUNAN, Michael J. (1929-)

Born County Limerick

DLA (IPA, 1963)

Clerical Officer, Limerick County Council, 1948-63
Staff Officer, Limerick County Council, 1963-69
County Accountant, Leitrim County Council, 1969-72
Senior Administrative Officer, Dublin County Council, 1972
County Secretary, Carlow County Council, 1972-78
Cork Assistant County Manager, 1978-83

Roscommon County Manager, 1983-84
Clare County Manager, 1984-

Director, Craggaunowen Project, 1984-

O'BRIEN, Francis J. (1927-)

Born County Meath

DLA (IPA, 1965)

Clerical Officer, Trim UDC, 1947-48
Temporary Town Clerk, Trim UDC, 1948-50

Clerk, Torc Manufacturing Co, Ltd, Trim, 1951

Town Clerk, Buncrana UDC, 1951-59
Town Clerk, Ballinasloe UDC, 1959-64
Town Clerk, Drogheda Corporation, 1964-68
County Secretary, Westmeath County Council, 1968-71
Cork Assistant County Manager, 1971-73

Wicklow County Manager, 1973-76

Meath County Manager, 1976-

Member, Executive Committee, Association of Municipal Authorities of Ireland, 1959-64
Member, Executive Committee, Institute of Public Administration, 1974-80

Chairman, International Urban Technology Exchange Programme Ltd, (IUTEP), 1982-86
Chairman, County and City Managers' Association, 1982-84
Chairman, Local Government Staff Negotiations Board, 1983-85
Director, Foras Forbartha and Chairman, Planning Division, 1983-87
Director, Youth Employment Agency, 1986-87
Member, Editorial Board, *Environmental Science*, 1986-87
Member, Industrial Development Authority Dublin and East Regional Small Industries Board, 1987-89

Ó BROLCHÁIN, Ruairí (1913-   )

Born Dublin city

BA (UCD, 1934)

Deputy Staff Officer, National Health Insurance Society, Dublin, 1934-44

County Secretary, Mayo County Council, 1944-46
Tipperary (NR and SR) Assistant County Manager, 1946-48

Meath County Manager, 1948-57
Dublin Assistant City and County Manager, 1957-78

Honorary Secretary and Treasurer, County and City Managers' Association, 1947-57
Director, National Mass-radiography Association, 1951-53
Chairman, Institute of Public Administration, 1960-61
Chairman, Local Government Computer Services Board, 1975-78

Consultant to Local Government Computer Services Board, 1978-82
Chairman, Board of National College of Art and Design, 1981-84

Ó CONCHUBHAIR, Cathal (1914-83)

Born Waterford city

Solicitor (1980)

Assistant, Messrs. Ranks (Ireland) Ltd, 1934-38
Chief Clerk, Messrs. Ranks (Ireland) Ltd, 1938-48

Town Clerk, Ceannanus Mor UDC, 1948-50
Town Clerk, New Ross UDC, 1950
Town Clerk, Enniscorthy UDC, 1950-51
County Accountant, Mayo County Council, 1951-56
County Secretary, Roscommon County Council, 1956-57
County Secretary, Meath County Council, 1957-66

Waterford County Manager, 1966-79

Temporary Waterford County Manager, 1979-80

In practice as solicitor in Tramore, 1980-83

O'CONNOR, Matthew J. (1934-)

Born County Kildare

DLA (IPA, 1971)
BA (UCC, 1983)

Draughtsman, Office of Public Works, Tullamore,
1953-54

Clerical Officer, Offaly County Council, 1954-64
Town Clerk, Birr UDC, 1965-66
Staff Officer, Limerick Corporation, 1966-72
Town Clerk, Dungarvan UDC, 1972-73
Section Officer, Cork Corporation, 1973-74

Senior Executive Officer/Hospital Administrator, Western Health
Board, 1974-80

Assistant Town Clerk, Cork Corporation, 1980-84
Assistant City Manager, Cork Corporation, 1984-90

Carlow County Manager, 1990-

Member, Industrial Development Authority South East Region Small
Industries Board, 1990-

O'CONNOR, Thomas M. (1911-)

Born County Tipperary

DPA (UCD, 1945)
BA (UCD, 1946)

Employment Clerk, Department of Industry and Commerce, 1934-47

Staff Officer, Dublin Board of Assistance, 1947-48
Town Clerk, Ballinasloe UDC, 1948-51
Town Clerk, Sligo Corporation, 1951-55
County Secretary, Westmeath County Council, 1955-60
Galway Assistant County Manager, 1960-62

Limerick County Manager, 1963-69
(Seconded to Industrial Development Authority to organise the Small Industries Programme, 1967-69)

Director, Mid-Western Regional Tourism Organisation Ltd, 1965-67

Manager, Grade I, later Secretary and Administration Manager, Industrial Development Authority, 1969-76
Part-time, Development Cooperation Division, Industrial Development Authority, 1976-78

Member, Executive Committee, Trocaire, 1973-80
Founder Member, State Agencies Development Cooperation Organisation (DEVCO), 1974, and member, Executive Committee, 1974-78
Founder Member, Confederation of Non-Governmental Organisations for Overseas Development (CONGOOD), 1975
Member, Irish delegation, Euro-Arab Dialogue (meetings in Cairo, Rome, Abu Dhabi and Brussels), 1975-78
Member, Council and Executive Committee, Agency for Personal Service Overseas (APSO), 1976-82

Founder, board member and first Chairman, Retirement Planning Council, 1976-
Member, National Council for the Aged (now the National Council for the Elderly), 1981-89
Member, Irish delegation, United Nations World Assembly on Aging, Vienna, 1982
Chairman, Dun Laoghaire Area Committee, Rehabilitation Institute, 1985-
Board Member, L'Arche Ireland, 1986-89
Board Member, Rehabilitation Institute, 1986-
Board Member, Housing Association for Integrated Living, 1986-

Author, *The Irish Experience in Export Oriented Industrial Development*, a case-study commissioned by the United Nations Industrial Development Organisation, 1975

O'DOHERTY, Joseph (1891-1979)

Born County Derry

Barrister-at-law (The King's Inns, Dublin, 1936)

Member, GHQ Staff, Irish Volunteers, 1917-18
Member, National Executive, Irish Volunteers, 1918-21
Member, Irish Republican Delegation to the USA, 1922-24 and 1924-26
Member, Dáil Éireann, 1918-27 and 1933-37
Member, Seanad Éireann, 1928-33

In practice at the Bar, 1936-45

Carlow-Kildare County Manager, 1945-57

Postscript to letter dated 7 September 1922 from Eamon de Valera, enclosed with letter of same date addressed to Cathal O Murchadha (Charles Murphy, ex-TD) authorising him to read it 'for the party' in advance of the meeting of the Dáil on 9 September:

> 5. American Delegation. I agree with Austin [Stack, TD] that it is only the Clann and such friends who are likely to be approachable or of any value at the moment. If Seán T. [Ó Ceallaigh, TD] is released he would be the very best in my opinion. If Sceilg [J.J. O'Kelly, TD] is prepared to go, as he has been over the ground before, he would be the next best. Joe Doherty would certainly be a very good companion.

(*Correspondence of Mr Eamon de Valera and Others:* published by Dáil Éireann (Pairlimint Shealadach), 1922.)
As will be noted above, Mr O'Doherty was a member of the delegation.

Mr O'Doherty, speaking in Dáil Éireann on 7 January 1922:

> ... I have my ideals of the people's will and at this stage of the proceedings I have no intention of saying anything bitter about any man or body of men in this assembly ... it is not a question of tweedeldum and tweedledee... It is the great question of Irish sovereignty, and as long as I have a weapon to fight for that cause I shall not be a party to voting away the sovereignty of this nation *(applause).*

(*Iris Dháil Éireann: Official Report, Debate on the Treaty between Great Britain and Ireland:* Talbot Press, Dublin 1922, page 323)

O'FLYNN, Clement I. (1900-)

Born Limerick city

ACCA (1925)
FACCA (1938)

Employee (Accountancy and Correspondence), Irish Co-Operative Agency Society Ltd, Limerick, 1919-25
Employee (Financial and Cost Accounts), Irish BP Co. Ltd, Limerick, 1925-28

County Accountant, Limerick County Council, 1928-31
County Secretary, Galway County Council, 1931-42

County Commissioner, Galway, 1940-42

Galway County Manager, 1942-65

Temporary Galway County Manager, 1965-66

Member, National Health Council, 1953-58
Chairman, County and City Managers' Association, 1956-57
Director, Bord na Mona, 1965-72
Honorary Life Member, Galway Chamber of Commerce, 1966

Ó GIOLLÁIN, Seán (1909-)

Born County Mayo

BA (NUI, 1932)
H Dip in Ed (UCD, 1933)
Diploma in Library Training (UCD, 1933)

Clerk and Assistant Cashier, Irish Press Ltd, 1934-36
Secondary Teacher, Christian Brothers School, Dingle, 1936-45

Superintendent Assistance Officer, Galway County Council, 1945-46
Town Clerk, Athlone UDC, 1947-48
Town Clerk, Galway Corporation, 1948-59

Waterford City Manager, 1959-66
Roscommon County Manager, 1966-74

Temporary Roscommon County Manager, 1974-75

Member, UCG Board of Extra-Mural Studies, 1973-75

Financial Controller, Messrs P.J. Tobin, Consulting Engineers, Galway, 1975-81

O'HALLORAN, Patrick (1918-68)

Born Cork city

BA (UCC, 1943)

Employment Clerk, Department of Social Welfare, 1939-48

Staff Officer, Tipperary (SR) County Council, 1948-54
Chief Clerk, Clonmel Mental Hospital Board, 1954-57
(Seconded as Organisation and Methods Officer, Tipperary (NR and SR) County Councils, 1956-57)
County Secretary, Wexford County Council, 1957-59

Kerry County Manager, 1959-68

O'KEEFFE, David (1887-1966)

Born County Cork

Clerical Assistant, progressing to County Accountant, Cork County Council, 1906-21
Local Government Auditor, Department of Local Government and Public Health, 1921-42

Commissioner, Offaly County Council and Offaly Board of Health and Public Assistance, 1924-28
Commisioner, Leitrim Board of Health and Public Assistance, 1938-42

County Commissioner, Leitrim, 1940-42

Commissioner, Clare Board of Health and Public Assistance, 1942 (22 April-25 August)
Commissioner, Clare County Council, 1942-45

Deemed to be Clare County Manager, 1942-45*

Clare County Manager, 1945-48

103

* The members of Clare County Council were removed from office on 22 April 1942 and David O'Keeffe was appointed Commissioner. By virtue of Section 5 (1) (c) of the County Management (Amendment) Act 1942, he was deemed to be County Manager (from 26 August 1942) until the suspension of the County Council had ceased, but not the first County Manager under the County Management Act 1940.

O'MAHONY, Timothy C. (1900-)

Born County Kerry

Accountant to J.K. O'Connor & Sons, P.H. McElligott & Sons and W.H.O'Connor (Castleisland and Dublin); Press Correspondent (part-time), Kerryman Newspapers, 1918-26
Chief Clerk, H. Coleman and Co., Public Auditors, Dublin, 1926-27

Superintendent Assistance Officer, Kerry Board of Health and Public Assistance, 1927-30
Town Clerk, Dundalk UDC, 1930-35
County Secretary, Leitrim County Council and Secretary, Leitrim Board of Health and Public Assistance, 1935

Limerick City Manager, 1936-38
Dun Laoghaire Borough Manager, 1938-42
Dublin Assistant City and County Manager, 1942-58
(Appointed by Section 10 (4) of the County Management Act 1940)
(Director of Housing, Dublin City and County, 1948)

Dublin City and County Manager, 1958-65

Commissioner, Bray UDC, 1969-70

O'MALLEY, Michael J. (1928-89)

Born County Mayo

Temporary Assistant County Engineer, Mayo County Council, 1952

Junior Engineer, Bord na Mona, 1952

Temporary Assistant County Engineer, Clare County Council, 1952-55
Resident Engineer, Meath County Council, 1955-56
Resident Engineer, Wicklow County Council, 1956
Temporary Assistant County Engineer, Wexford County Council, 1956-59

Temporary Assistant County Engineer, Kildare County Council, 1959-61
Assistant County Engineer, Donegal County Council, 1961-66
Chief Assistant County Engineer, Donegal County Council, 1966-70
Chief Assistant County Engineer (Planning), Donegal County Council, 1970-71
Deputy County Engineer, Donegal County Council, 1971-73
County Engineer, Carlow County Council, 1973-76

Mayo County Manager, 1976-89

Member, Dublin Transportation Commission, 1978-80
Chairman, Udaras na Gaeltachta, 1980-83
Member, Industrial Development Authority West Region Small Industries Board, 1985-89

QUINLAN, William F. (1895-1971)

Born County Kerry

Solicitor (1918)

Solicitor, Tralee, 1918-19

County Secretary, Kerry County Council, 1919-30
County Secretary and County Solicitor, Kerry County Council, 1930-32
County Secretary, Kerry County Council, 1932-42

County Commissioner, Kerry, 1940-42

Kerry County Manager, 1942-58
(Seconded to Irish Tourist Board as Chairman, 1949-50)

First Chairman, County and City Managers' Association, 1943-47

QUINLIVAN, John (1938-)

Born Limerick city

DPA (IPA, 1968)
Diplomas in Economics, Accounting and Legal Studies (School of Accountancy, Glasgow, 1973)

105

Clerical Officer, Limerick Corporation, 1955-58
Time Keeper/Weightmaster, Limerick Corporation, 1959-60
Gas Slot Meter Collector, Limerick Corporation, 1960-65
Rent Collector, Limerick Corporation, 1966
Town Clerk, Cashel UDC, 1966-68
Town Clerk, Athy UDC, 1968-69
Town Clerk, Castlebar UDC, 1969-73
Town Clerk, Carlow UDC, 1973-78
Town Clerk, Dundalk UDC, 1978-79
County Secretary, Laois County Council, 1979-83
Wexford Assistant County Manager, 1983-88

Louth County Manager, 1988-

Member, Newry and Mourne and Dundalk Joint Committee for Cross
Border Activities, 1988-
Member, East Border Region Committee (for counties Louth, Monaghan,
Down and Armagh), 1988-
Member, Industrial Development Authority North East
Region Small Industries Board, 1988-
Patron, Carlingford Lough Heritage Trust, 1990-

RAFTIS, Liam (1887-1960)

Born Waterford city

Clerk, Great Southern Railways, 1905-20

Borough Treasurer and Estate Agent, Waterford Corporation, 1920-45

Waterford City Manager, 1945-59

Chairman, County and City Managers' Association, 1954-55

RICE, Thomas P. (1934-)

Born Dublin city

DPA (UCD, 1955)
Certificate in Government Accountancy and Finance (School of
Commerce, Rathmines, Dublin, 1957)

Temporary Clerical Officer, Dublin Corporation, 1952

Executive Officer, Department of Local Government, 1952-60
(Organisation and Methods Officer, Department of Local Government, 1957-58)
Higher Executive Officer, Department of Local Government, 1960-65
Assistant Principal Officer, Department of Local Government, 1965-71

County Secretary, Tipperary (NR) County Council, 1971-74
Cork Assistant County Manager, 1974-76

Tipperary (SR) County Manager, 1976-83
Limerick City Manager, 1983-87
Cork City Manager, 1987-

Member, Board of Co-operation North, 1979-
Chairman, Local Government Computer Services Board, 1985-86
Member, Industrial Development Authority South West Region Small Industries Board, 1987-

SHARKEY, Austin A. (1919-84)

Born County Mayo

Clerical Officer, Offaly County Council, 1936-50
Secretary of Barrow Drainage Board and of six Joint Drainage Committees, 1946-50
Staff Officer, Dublin County Council, 1950-56
Organisation and Methods Officer, Dublin County Council, 1956-58
Senior Staff Officer, Dublin County Council, 1958-59
County Secretary, Donegal County Council, 1959-66

Galway County Manager, 1966-72
Meath County Manager, 1973-75

SHERLOCK, Gerald J. (1876-1942)

Born Dublin city

Junior Clerk, Chief Clerk in City Engineer's Office, Manager, Dublin Waterworks and Assistant Town Clerk, Dublin Corporation, 1894-1927
Town Clerk, Dublin Corporation, 1927-30

Dublin City Manager, 1930-36
(Appointed by Section 53 (1) of the Local Government (Dublin)
Act 1930)

SINNOTT, Thomas D. (1893-1965)

Born County Wexford

Teacher, St Vincent's Orphanage, Glasnevin, Dublin, 1911-12
Teacher, Christian Brothers' School, Dundalk, 1912-14
Teacher, Christian Brothers' School, Enniscorthy, 1914-16
Manager of own business, Enniscorthy, 1917
Teacher, Christian Brothers' School, Enniscorthy, 1917-18 and
1919-20

Secretary, Wexford Board of Health and Public Assistance, 1922-42

County Commissioner, Wexford, 1940-42

Wexford County Manager, 1942-53

Chairman, Enniscorthy Board of Guardians, 1920-22

Joined Irish Volunteers, 1914
Appointed Officer, Irish Volunteers, 1916
Periodic imprisonment and internment in Ballykinlar Camp, Cork Jail,
Frongoch Jain, Kilworth Camp, and Waterford Jail, 1916-21

While interned in Frongoch Jail, he was one of the five Camp leaders.
He was tried with Richard Mulcahy by Field General Courtmartial for
leading the prisoners' mutiny which brought about the general release of
Christmas 1916.

TAAFFE, John A. (1933-)

Born County Mayo

DPA (IPA, 1970)
FCIS (1974)

Temporary Clerk, Bord na Mona, 1952

108

Meeting of the County and City Managers' Association, 18 October 1990, Ennis: (Front row, l-r) M. Deigan, Laois County Manager, S. Keating, Galway, F. O'Brien, Meath, G. Ward, Kildare, P. Donnelly, Kilkenny, T. Rice, Cork City, M. Nunan, Clare. (Middle row, l-r) J. Higgins, Limerick City, J. Quinlivan, Louth, S. McCarthy, Offaly, B. Treacy, Wicklow, P. Doyle, Leitrim, M. Doody, Waterford City, J. Prendergast, Dublin Assistant City & County Manager, P. Morrissey, Dublin Assistant City & County Manager, B. Johnston, Cavan County Council. (Back row, l-r) M. Killeen, Longford, J. McGinley, Tipperary (NR), J. Gavin, Monaghan, M. O'Connor, Carlow, D. Mahon, Mayo, S. Hayes, Tipperary (SR), D. Connolly, Roscommon, S. Murphy, Limerick, J. Taaffe, Westmeath.

Clerical Officer, Laois County Council, 1952-54
Clerical Officer, Kildare County Council, 1954-63
Staff Officer, Carlow County Council, 1963-64
Staff Officer, Kildare County Council, 1964-70
Town Clerk, Tullamore UDC, 1970-72
County Accountant, Roscommon County Council, 1972-73
County Accountant, Laois County Council, 1973-74
County Secretary, Laois County Council, 1974-78
Mayo Assistant County Manager, 1978-81

Westmeath County Manager, 1981-

TREACY, Blaise (1935-)

Born Dublin city

Diploma in Local Administration (IPA, 1965)

Clerical Officer, Kildare County Council, 1952-58
Organisation and Methods Officer, Kildare County Council, 1958-59
Assistant Clerk, Carlow Mental Hospital Board, 1959-60
Town Clerk, Carrickmacross UDC, 1960-63
Superintendent Assistance Officer, Cavan County Council, 1963-66
Staff Officer, Carlow UDC, 1966-67
Town Clerk, Carlow UDC, 1967-73
Town Clerk, Dundalk UDC, 1973-74
County Secretary, Kerry County Council, 1974-78
Clare Assistant County Manager, 1978-85

Wicklow County Manager, 1985-

Member, Arklow Enterprise Council, 1987-
Director and Founder Member, Wicklow County Tourism Company Ltd,
1987-
Member, Tiglin (Adventure Centre, Ashford) Advisory Committee,
1989-
Member, Industrial Development Authority Dublin and East Regional
Small Industries Board, 1989-
Board Member, Horizon Radio (North Wicklow Community
Broadcasting Co-Operative Society Ltd), 1989-
Member, Cospoir, 1990-

VEALE, Michael A. (1903-70)

Born Waterford city

Clerk, Great Southern Railways, 1920-35

Town Clerk, Carrick-on-Suir UDC, 1935-37
Secretary, Cavan Board of Health and Public Assistance, 1937-42

Cavan County Manager, 1942-45
Laois-Offaly County Manager, 1945-57
Dublin Assistant City and County Manager, 1957-68

Temporary Dublin Assistant City and County Manager, 1968-69

Member, National Health Council, 1953-58
Chairman, County and City Managers' Association, 1957-60

WARD, John G. (1928-)

Born Derry city

DLA (IPA, 1964)

Substitute teacher, Letterbrick NS, Cloghan, County
Donegal, 1947-48

Clerical Officer, Donegal County Council, 1948-53
Staff Officer, Donegal County Council, 1954-62
County Accountant, Limerick County Council, 1962-67
County Secretary, Leitrim County Council, 1967-71

Mayo County Manager, 1971-75
Kildare County Manager, 1975-

Chairman, Leitrim County Development Team, 1967-71
Member, Industrial Development Authority, Dublin and East Regional
Small Industries Board, 1985-87
Chairman, County and City Managers' Association, 1988-90
Chairman, Institute of Public Administration, 1990-

111

WILLIAMS, Desmond (1915-)

Born Dublin city

Corporation of Accountants Final Examination, 1937
DPA (UCD, 1945)
BComm (UCD, 1947)

Junior Clerk, Dublin Corporation, 1932-36
Class B Clerk, Dublin Corporation, 1936-40
Class A Clerk, Dublin Corporation, 1940-47
(Seconded to Monaghan County Council as temporary County
Accountant, 1946)
County Accountant, Carlow County Council, 1947-48
County Accountant, Dublin County Council, 1949-55
(Temporary County Secretary, Dublin County Council, 1950-55)
Cork Assistant County Manager, 1955-58

Donegal County Manager, 1958-80

President, St Columba's Branch, National Council for the Blind, 1959-88
Director, National Mass-radiography Association, 1966-68
Chairman, Executive Committee, Donegal Historical Society, 1974-
Chairman, County and City Managers' Association, 1976-77
President, Donegal Historical Society, 1977-80
Member, Board of Co-Operation North, 1979-85
Member, Council of Co-Operation North, 1979-

Life member, International City Management Association, 1980

Member, Advisory Committee of Highland Radio, 1990

Author, *Donegal County Council: 75 Years, 1899-1974*

WRENNE, Joseph F. (1888-1966)

Born County Cork

BA (UCC, 1915)
MA (UCC, 1916)

Professor of History, University College Cork, 1918-21

Clerical Assistant, Office of County Secretary, Cork County Council, 1906-25
Chief Clerk, Roads Department, Cork County Council, 1925-32
County Secretary, Cork County Council, 1932-42

Cork County Manager, 1942-54

Mr Wrenne wrote three full-length plays. One of these, *Sable and Gold* (written under the pseudonym Maurice Dalton), was first performed in the Father Matthew Hall, Cork, 15 May 1918. It played the same year for three weeks in the Abbey Theatre, Dublin. It was published by Maunsel and Roberts in 1918. Mr Wrenne was an Oireachtas prize-winner for Irish essay and original short story in Irish.

V
SILHOUETTE:
PHILIP MONAHAN

How Troy fell Aeneas tells Dido in the second book of the *Aeneid*. The Greeks left their horse filled with armed men and slipped down the Dardanelles as if at last for home. In the lee of Tenedos, twelve miles away, they dropped anchor and waited. Tenedos, treacherous anchorage for ships — *statio mala fida carinis*. This phrase Cork with native ambivalence transmuted into the civic motto *statio bene fida carinis*: the treacherous has been dubbed secure.

Those who, reversing another legend, move from Dublin to Cork have two minds on whether the anchorage is treacherous or secure. Who leaving the vulgar thrust of Dublin (one writes of relatives, not absolutes) will not be enchanted by the beauty, the unhurried grace, the charm, the intelligence of Cork; and who, through the tough skin of his Dublin smugness, has not felt the keen cut of that charming, intense, deadly intelligence, the cut that wounds as deeply as a blade-edge of grass. There is an art in surviving there, like that of the bull ring. Not every bull comes to terms with the deadly skill, the smiling virtuosity, the graceful tautness of the *torero*. There are bulls who improbably have become as Ferdinand, and there are bulls who, defiant like MacConglinne, have met in Cork the moment of truth. This study is of a third kind of animal, naughty enough to defend himself, to master and survive.

To live unfrustrated in Ireland calls, according to the books, for skill; in Cork it is an art, for here the taut is treacherous and the secure is, in the existential sense, absurd. Seán O'Faoláin, who grew to manhood there and who like so many has written lovingly and beautifully of her, anchored thereon his *Irish Journey*. He brooded on her deadly smiling power, and appraised her as a beauty, a bore and a bitch.

When the Cork City Management Act, 1929, was before the Dáil the late Hugo Flinn said that to deny Cork the right to appoint her own city manager and to appoint Philip Monahan by statute was the difference between free marriage and "forced permanent concubinage for the rest of his natural life for this designated bridegroom of Cork." The Oireachtas was not deterred from legalising the union. Five years before this formidable bride had been delivered to Monahan by means, it has been suggested, not unlike those that led Diomede to master Troy. Whatever the origins, the legal union has now lasted twenty-five years and famous has been its progeny. This year we celebrate the silver jubilee of the civil marriage of the Cork bride to the Dublin unicorn, a marriage that began one of the most striking administrative experiments of our time.

It gives a malicious delight to Dubliners to see this jealous city so long in the power of one of themselves. Philip Monahan was born, son of a commercial traveller of Baggot Street, in 1894 and educated by the Christian Brothers in Westland Row and North Richmond Street. He won a scholarship to University College, Dublin, and for three years studied science, but did not take a degree. Instead, in 1915, he became a secondary teacher in the Christian Brothers' School in Drogheda. This career, much interrupted by other activities, ended over thirty years ago but there are some who claim to trace the aura of the schoolmaster still faintly about him.

Outside school there was other drill. In 1916 he was head of the Drogheda branch of the Volunteers. They obeyed the order countermanding the Rising and thus did not share the hazards of the band from the rival town, Dundalk, who on the way to Dublin skirmished with the police. For this their leader, then known as John McEntee, was sentenced to death. Monahan was arrested in Dublin and interned with the rest. After the general release he went back to his job, but also threw himself into Sinn Fein politics as organiser and lecturer. He was soon in trouble and in Lincoln Jail. There is a story that for exercise he wrestled with a fellow prisoner, likewise a peccant schoolmster, Eamon de Valera, exercise not unworthy to be remembered with Jacob's.

For some the purple, for others the striped pants. For long the dilemma of good government or self government has been posed. It was an axiom of Sinn Fein to deny the dilemma and to assert that self government *was* good government. Who better to prove this than a young school teacher and where better to prove it than at one's doorstep, in the ancient borough of Drogheda? An issue was at hand. An enthusiastic local government auditor had charged a member of the Drogheda Corporation with some loss (the story is that it had to do with a venerable practice of the Corporation to facilitate Laytown races) and he refused to pay. The matter degenerated (or was elevated?) into comedy; the bailiff sent to seize the offender's pony and trap was outwitted when the pony's harness was found to be borrowed. This unpromising bit of comedy was worked into a campaign issue by Monahan and his men: old style abuses must be swept away and old style representatives with them. He campaigned with the Auditor's report in his hands and the 1920 election saw the victory of Sinn Fein in Drogheda, with Monahan its

117

leading representative there elected both a member of the Louth County Council and Mayor of the borough at the age of twenty-six. The victory was significant, not only because Drogheda's allegiance was swung from the Local Government Board, for that was happening generally, but also for the nature of the campaign that applied the widest idealism to the narrowest issues: it was the shape of the decade to come. It was significant too in that perhaps not before or since has a local government auditor been so bravely vindicated, and this one was E.P. McCarron who became the first Secretary of the Department of Local Government and Public Health.

When the split came Monahan took the Treaty side, and was seriously wounded in Drogheda trying to prevent a clash between opposing forces.

The new Government, faced with the disorganisation caused by the efforts to dislodge the old régime, the effects of the civil war, a serious agricultural slump, and the lassitude of the citizens in the matter of rate-paying, required powers to discipline incompetent or neglectful councils. They got these in March 1923 when the Local Government (Temporary Provisions) Act became law. Local representative institutions toppled fast, twenty of them in twenty-one months, their affairs entrusted to officers of the Minister. They ranged from great bodies like the Dublin and Cork corporations to the Mohill Rural District Council. First to fall was the Kerry County Council, followed within a month by the Kerry County Board of Health. At the present time a public servant charged with an unpleasant job may expect at worst to be publicly denigrated, but Kerry in the first half of 1923 was not to be trifled with, and those who did so might well be rewarded with one of the gorgeous State funerals of the time. If Kerry were to be held it must be with an economy of civil servants' lives. This, it is said, made the Minister, Ernest Blythe, look for a more expendable person to appoint to this first and most dangerous of commissionerships. Perhaps some memory of the auditor's report was at work, for a most unusual step was taken. The Mayor of Drogheda, Philip Monahan, was summoned, given twenty-four hours, and sent to Kerry in May, 1923. The public representative was become a public servant, strange apprenticeship for the career to come.

In 1923 also Monahan married, and has one daughter. He spent just over a year in Kerry; both parties emerged scathless from the experience, Monahan (in the bureaucratic disguise of P. O'Muineacháin, which he

118

still affects) not without honour, because in the latter part of 1924 he begins to be entrusted with control of one local authority in Cork after another. The West Cork County Board of Health, Cork Corporation, Cobh Urban District Council, South Cork County Board of Public Assistance, Cork District Mental Hospital Committee, fell at one time or another into his hands; it reads like a military progress. This was strange behaviour for a Mayor, to trample in this way on representative institutions; but he had become a Mayor to show that the new Ireland had a passion for good, efficient, administration and now was opened up to him a field where these qualities were needed and could be used. The representative must become the administrator. The emotion that had gone before was spent, or a little sour: the burning heart must give way to the cool head. After all these years Ireland had been restored to her people; what they must show was that in restoring order, in the practical discharge of affairs, in applying ruthless common sense her people could rise to the challenge of the time. This was the famous realism of the 'twenties, and few men have been more finely tempered by it than Philip Monahan or have more brilliantly exemplified it in their work.

In the latter part of 1924, apparently at the request of a group of Cork citizens, an Inspector of the Department held a local inquiry and reported that the duties of the Corporation had not been effectively discharged and the conquering Mr. Monahan, aged 30, arrived with an order in his pocket banishing the 56 members of the Council and their fifteen committees: their duties were entrusted to him: the Lord Protector was taking over. It was the end of a chapter, for while the Kerry County Council and the rest that had fallen to him would regain for a good period their full powers, the Cork City Council never would.

There was plenty to do. The city finances were in a sad state, a deficit of £75,000 at end of March, 1924, on the current accounts of a city whose valuation was £180,000 and all the current accounts and some of the capital accounts in the red. The streets were bad. In summer raw river water was supplied for domestic use. Old rubble masonry tunnels took the place of sewers and discharged undiluted sewage into the river. In the principal streets these tunnels were collapsing beneath the weight of traffic. The Corporation, since the burning of the City Hall, had no proper accommodation and the discharge of business was much impeded.

New offices were at once provided. Superfluous staff at the Municipal Markets were sacked, and a trading loss there turned into a tidy profit. Wages of Corporation employees were cut from 62/6 a week in 1924 to 56/- a week in 1927 and by a further 2/- a week in the following year. £50,000 was borrowed in 1925 to asphalt the principal streets, and the work was done in six months. Better streets, acceptance of lowest tenders and general re-organisation cut the cost of the street cleansing and domestic scavenging by £11,000 a year, or one third. £25,000 was spent on making the water supply safe. The money paid in compensation for the burned City Hall was diverted to building 150 houses on the house purchase principle, the tidy sum of £14,000 being collected in deposits on these and spent to build more houses. Solvency was restored, substantial improvements were made in the city and the rates fell 1/11d. in the pound, or by just 10%. As so often, good service and economy went hand in hand. This was the work of almost two years. The remaining period of his commissionership was devoted to more housebuilding, more sewers, better scavenging, overhaul of the health and veterinary services, as well as to more routine matters. Already by 1928 his report in the Department's annual report for 1927-28 betrays a note of weariness and a desire perhaps for fresh woods: "There is little to report....It will be readily realised that a Commissioner's work must become somewhat routine in character as the more obvious defects of the old régime are remedied."

It seemed clear to thinking men at the time from this and other experience that the old system of local government could not survive but it was as clear that local government by commissioner could not indefinitely continue. The Greater Dublin Commission in 1926 and a local committee of Cork citizens set up in the same year recommended a system of city management for the two cities. The Poor Law Commission in 1928 recommended county management, for poor law work. The management system, adapted from the American system of city management, seemed to offer a synthesis of what was best in the representative and the commissioner systems. The discharge of business would be in the hands of a competent official, while the overall control would rest with the elected representative. Early in 1928 the Minister travelled to Cork and consulted with representative citizens and some months later introduced the Cork City Management Bill under which Philip Monahan was made Cork City Manager for life. The American system in being translated to a different legal and administrative environment was given a rigid legal basis. It was a time it will be recalled of great experiment — public assistance on a county basis and the end of the guardians in 1923, the end of rural districts in 1925, the setting up of combined purchasing in the same year, the founding of an efficiently recruited and mobile local service under the Acts of 1923, 1925 and 1926, the ruthless cleaning up of inefficiency from 1923, and now management. It was a time of ideas, vigour and action.

The 'twenties is a decade fascinating now to look back upon for its virtues as for its failings. How strange in these inflationary times to read of wages being cut, proudly it seems from £3.2.6. a week to £2.14.0: Cork was not exceptional in this — the Dublin Commissioners were doing the same; for this was the period of deflation, the pre-war value of the pound was being restored (wages under Cork Corporation before 1914 were 18/- per week). There could be pipe dreams too — another distinguished import to Cork, Dr. Alfred O Rahilly, published during those years a pamphlet to show how income tax might be abolished. The energy with which Monahan attacked abuses and the speed with which services were improved, the pride in sound finance, the building of houses to buy not to let, the glory in economical administration these are the marks not only of the man but of the time, when the supreme value was clear headed courageous efficiency. These conservative standards have been much out of fashion in our times, but a standard can have its value out of fashion as in. Who is to say that two or three decades hence it will not be our standards that will be obscured and those of the 'twenties restored? Hard-headedness has a way of surviving. One sees in Monahan a conscious detachment from the times but there is no doubt an unconscious factor also at work. The 'twenties were his "marvellous years" and nothing that has come since then can have had the same savour. From 1920 to 1929 he embodied the humane, practical idealism of these years at their best. He is in a real sense one of the last as well as one of the most notable survivals of what to him cannot but seem to be a golden time.

These are qualities admired but not loved, and Monahan true to his time has not sought to be judged by other standards of other times. A city or a county manager works in a public world but as part of the organisation he serves; in Cork one gets the impression that the organisation is overshadowed by the public personality of the manager.

Thus, in Dublin one will be told that the Corporation does such and such; but in Cork one is told that it is *Monahan's* doing. Even for a small town this pervasiveness is striking: he is part of the living city, partly because he is to be seen constantly about it. The stories are revealing. There is the famous, if apocryphal, one of his coming on two labourers opening a street. They are idle and impertinent, and he dismisses them, then learns they work for the Gas Company. And another, that in the mornings he observes how each district's scavenging goes. These dramatise his strong sense of personal responsibility, a quality easier to practice in the twenties when public organisations were small than now when they have grown so large as either to blunt the edge of personal responsibility or, by demanding new methods of control, make its practice anachronistic. Thus one gets the impression from afar that the handsome new City Hall contains a staff of two, the manager and a typist, that each morning he opens the post and there and then, without tedious file-mongering, dictates the replies, brief, devastating and, occasionally, slightly of the beam, and that they are signed and dispatched that evening — Monahan *contra mundum*. This may be businesslike and the way they worked in the 'twenties, but we have moved on since then, to a state of what Father Fergal McGrath has brilliantly described as "highly organised procrastination." The Government Department, for example, that delivers itself after due gestation of a ponderous missive and is laconically and unhelpfully replied to by return may occasionally feel that Monahan's letter are like life in Hobbes's state of nature — nasty, brutish and short. Seriously, the public personality that emerges is of an independent, brusque, perhaps impetuous official who carries in his head the detailed affairs of his city, of a manager fully in control. Some critics suggest that management was devised to staff the local authorities with creatures of the Custom House. If so, a mighty poor selection was made for the first job of Manager.

Of course, the City Hall contains more officials than two (though fewer than practice elsewhere would lead one to suspect) and one of Monahan's striking successes has been in keeping his team pulling in the same general direction. Success of this kind, building unity on undisputed control, is not so frequent in the local service as to be taken for granted, and is not achieved without its ups and downs. During one of the downs two officers of the Corporation seldom together were seen swearing eternal fidelity. 'We are banded together,' one of them explained, 'against the common enemy — Phil.'

A notable, and characteristic, administrative advance can be ascribed to him: the institution in Cork, first in Ireland, of the new system of differential rents, under which the rent is related to the capacity to pay with the result that it is no longer necessary to fix the rent near what the poorest can pay. Under this system, while the poor are helped, a higher average rent can be collected. This has worked smoothly and successfully in Cork, and it was this success and Monahan's lucid and businesslike account of the scheme, in his evidence at the Dublin Housing Inquiry, that no doubt influenced the Report's emphatic recommendation in its favour for Dublin and that led to its being taken up after 1945 and adopted throughout the country.

After thirty years of his firm rule there are many citizens of Cork who feel strongly about him. To some he is the suave, efficient, hardworking public servant the city needs; to others he is unable or unwilling to keep up with the times, an autocrat, immoveable. There is a story that once his car stalled on the Mardyke near his home. He was helped to put it by the pathway and an onlooker watching him walk away said "That's the first time I ever saw the manager pushed off the road." For some he has done the city great material good, for others he has done it what, for want of a better word, might be called great spiritual harm. To some he is devoted to the city's service; to others he lacks the interest in its advancement that a native would have. The views may not all be mutually exclusive. Certainly, the Cork City Council, who for many years have worked contentedly with their manager, have in recent years raised voices of criticism of his failure to respond fully to the challenge of the city's housing problem. An old test of the success of a rule was whether the population rose — that of Cork has been static. There is a secular tendency to move from the centres of cities and live in the suburbs. Dublin has made several convulsive expansions of its boundary, but Cork has not done likewise, though an extension is now under way. The result has been that the cost of the capital and current expenditure involved by the growth of what the census calls the South West Suburbs, together with the increased rateable valuation, has fallen to Cork County Council, not to the ratepayers of Cork City. It this shrewd management or a cussed refusal to keep up with the times? It depends, does it not, on the point of view? To the feverish 'forties and 'fifties failure to respond to all challenge leads to breakdown; but the hard-headed 'twenties were more selective: gain and loss are to be nicely weighed. Monahan is nothing if not adroit and shrewd.

Whatever one's answer, it is clear that, to use a concept typical of our time, Monahan is *engaged* with Cork, and he emerges as a lonely, solitary figure, imperceptibly becoming estranged from our day, but master of the situation. For all that the public face bulks so large, the private face is almost unseen. The job of a city of county manager is essentially a lonely one — great authority is concentrated in him and, because the impact of local authorities is so wide and the freedom of action of a public servant so circumscribed, he must lead both in public and in private a life of great circumspection. If his daily job is done in the bright light his private life must be a twilight affair. Other types of public servant, especially those employed by large organisations in large cities, can sink into complete anonymity; but a manager in a small town has not this recourse. Thus, the Cork City Manager at a meeting of the Cork City Council has a presence and a dignity that in their way sublimate the youthful ideals of a man who began life as a teacher and began public life as a Mayor; but as a private individual, even after thirty years in Cork, he is almost unknown. A restaurant waitress said "He's the one person in Cork almost that I know nothing about. I don't know what circle he moves in or if he's married. They tell me he's the one to know if you want to get a house" (the unfailing barb!). A few glimpses can be collected: an evening drink with a single intimate in some pub near the Mall, in a corner screened by a large plant; a little indifferent golf; watching football, a boyhood love; some not indifferent poker; reading; charitable work — an epitome of the private life of almost any Irish public servant.

There is a puzzling contrast between the formidable correspondent and the suave, ready negotiator over the table. Here he is formidable still, in his ready grasp of a subject no matter how technical, in getting to the heart of the matter, in impatient suffering of fools, but quick, reasonable and practical in decision. While the pen is far from his hand he is a brilliant embodiment of the medieval tag that envisages the ideal administrator — *suaviter in modo, fortiter in re*, flexible in method, constant in principle.

He is, as befits the product of three cities and the prototype of city managers, notably urbane. Public servants are courteous and some have charm, but this quality of urbanity has a flavour of its own of an age older even than the 'twenties, difficult to convey in our terms but an authentic story may illustrate it. He attended, with other bureaucrats, the funeral of a colleague. As they were for home one well-known official was chaffed by the owners of the modest cars affected by bureaucrats on his pretensions in driving a large Dodge car. He defended himself with unquenchable enthusiasm, praising its astronomical mileage, its condition, its incredible economy on types and maintenance, its comfort and so on. This led to some inept jokes about the Artful Dodger but Monahan, who a few moments before had been plainly moved at the loss of a colleague and a friend, interposed in a quiet urbane tone. Taking as is characteristic with him his cigarette from his mouth with an upward gesture of his straightened hand, he said to the owner of the big car: 'You remind me, D.C., of the aphorism of John Morley, that politics is neither an art nor a science — it is a Dodge.'

Perhaps the most striking sign of his strength and his detachment from the life of the city he has served and managed for thirty years is his freedom from the infectious Cork accent: he speaks with the quiet unemphatic tones of the middle-class Dubliner — Monahan may have left his mark on Cork, but it has left on overt mark on him.

Talleyrand claimed as his contribution to the Revolution that he survived. "Cork" means a morass and Monahan far from being engulfed there has survived — as a Dubliner.

One can survive in Ireland on the model of a renaissance city prince, but to survive as a practical man doing practical things is the rub. 'What use is strength,' laments Samson eyeless at his mill, 'without a double share of wisdom?' The price of that double share is a heavy one and in Cork for thirty years a sore burden to bear, but hidden by Monahan under a cloak of urbane serenity. To O'Faoláin the conditions of success in Cork are "the skin of a rhinoceros, the dissimulation of a crocodile, the agility of a hare, the speed of a hawk." These, in the service of honest, hard-working purpose, make the notable public servant.

In pages such as these it is in the end the work rather than the man that is relevant and the work is there to assess. He is the first city manager. On the Cork model, management spread to Dublin, Dun Laoghaire, Limerick, Waterford, and then to all the counties. Monahan would be the first to deny that a legal framework has relevance to the success or failure of an institution such as management; but by the same reasoning on the success or failure of the Cork manager largely depended whether this most characteristic of our local government institutions would live and be extended, or die. Thus his service to Cork has had a significance far beyond the boundaries of the city. Most public servants work for forty years or so and have precious little to look back upon as their distinctive contribution to the society they have so long served. It is one of the rare rewards to put against the frustrations of the public service to look back upon a decisive contribution to some brave new administrative venture. The institution of management will, in Irish eyes, always be bound with the name of Philip Monahan.

One is left with the teasing thought that he who has been the prototype of the most characteristic administrative experiment of our age is still somewhat of an exile in our time, a survivor as it were from a lost age. He was given great authority young. He was thirty when he began to rule Cork and the cities and towns of the world must have seemed at his feet. Thirty years later he is still in Cork and the men and the values are changed. Only he is unchanged. Twenty-five years have passed since the civil marriage. It has had its troubles, but she has been a loyal wife, and he a steadfast, hardworking husband, and the fruits of their life together manifest and good. Perhaps it was a fortunate wind that brought his highbeaked ship to this long anchorage, where he who came to rule stayed to love, to feel for and with the place not as bricks and mortar but as flesh and blood, to be on fire, as one less wise, when she is scandalised. Could it be, when all is said, that Cork has proved it true that, at a price, she is *statio bene fida carinis*?

VI
A CHRONOLOGY OF LOCAL GOVERNMENT 1918-1990

Joseph Boland and Eunan O'Halpin

This chronology records significant events and developments for local authorities since 1918. Inevitably the compilers have had to be selective in the categories of material as well as the specific items included. National events which impinged on local government are recorded, while health matters are also dealt with until 1 April 1971, when the new area health boards took over all local authority health functions.

The only pre-1922 legislation included is the Local Government (Ireland) Act 1919, which provided for proportional representation in local authority elections, and the Government of Ireland Act 1920.

In many cases where a local authority was dissolved, subsidiary bodies also disappeared. In general, we do not list these. Furthermore, dissolutions of town commissioners are not recorded.

In order to avoid needless repetition, the title of the 'Minister for Local Government' is abbreviated to 'the Minister' after its first occurrence in the chronology.

In virtually every instance we have been able to trace the precise dates of the events recorded. Where two or more successive entries bear the same date, the date is not repeated.

1918

December 14	In the general election, Sinn Féin is the main victor, with 73 seats. The Nationalist Party wins only 6, the Unionists 25, and an Independent Unionist 1. The turnout is 69% in what is to be the last general election using the 'first past the post' voting system.

1919

January 15	The Ratepayers' Association heads the poll in the Sligo Corporation election, the first held in Ireland using PR/STV (under the Sligo Corporation Act of 1918). Sinn Féin is placed second.
January 21	Dáil Éireann meets for the first time, and declares itself the legitimate parliament of the Irish people.
April	The 'Municipal Officials (Ireland) Trade Union' is established. A year later it is renamed the 'Local Government (Ireland) Officials Trade Union'. It subsequently becomes the 'Irish Local Government Officials Union', and ultimately the 'Local Government and Public Services Union'.
April 2	The Dáil Ministry of Local Government is established, with W.T. Cosgrave, TD as its minister.

128

June 3	The Local Government (Ireland) Act 1919 provides for proportional representation at all local authority elections.
September 12	Dáil Éireann is declared illegal.

1920

January 15	Sinn Féin, with Nationalists and Labour, gain control of 172 out of 206 borough and urban district councils in elections.
January 30	Mayoral elections: Philip Monahan is elected mayor of Drogheda.
June	Elections of county councils, rural district councils and boards of guardians are held.
June 29	Dáil Éireann sets up a 'Commission of experts to enquire into the possibility of carrying on local administration without financial aid from the English Government'. Its chairman is Kevin O'Higgins TD, who on 26 August 1921 becomes the first and only Assistant Minister for Local Government.
August 12	The General Council of County Councils agrees in Dublin to hold meetings on 24 August in order to adopt the Commission's interim recommendations.
September 17	Dáil Éireann confirms the Commission's final report and orders that, as from 1 October 1920, the Dáil's Local Government Department will assume the authority and control hitherto exercised by the 'English Local Government Board'.
September 30	W.T. Cosgrave, the Minister, issues a circular to all Irish local authorities reiterating the Dáil's decree of 17 September, adding that it is 'unnecessary to remind the public bodies of Ireland that the fate of our Country is hanging in the balance', and that a favourable outcome partly depends on the 'energy, initiative and integrity of those who have been elected to control the internal administration of the country'.
December 23	The Government of Ireland Act 1920 provides for two subordinate Irish parliaments and administrations and a Council of Ireland for consultation on common interests.

129

1921

May 13 — Nomination day for general elections to the two parliaments established by the Government of Ireland Act 1920; all candidates nominated for election to the Southern Ireland parliament are returned unopposed (Sinn Féin 124, Independents 4).

May 25 — The Custom House, Dublin, the headquarters of the Local Government Board for Ireland since its establishment in 1872, is destroyed in an IRA attack: all the board's records are lost.

August 16 — Sinn Féin MPs elected to the Southern Ireland parliament convene in the Mansion House as the second Dáil Éireann.

December 6 — The Anglo-Irish Treaty is signed in London.

1922

January 7 — The Dáil approves the Anglo-Irish treaty by 64 votes to 57.

January 14 — The Dáil elects a Provisional Government of the Irish Free State with Michael Collins as its chairman.

March — The Provisional Government in one of its first decisions makes £1,000,000 available for urban housing, demonstrating concern for social improvement.

April 1 — E.P. McCarron is appointed secretary of the Local Government Department of the Provisional Government.

June 16 — In the 'Pact Election', the anti-treaty group suffers a major defeat. The results are: pro-treaty Sinn Féin 58, anti-treaty Sinn Féin 36, Labour 17, Farmers 7, Independents 10.

June 26 — The IRA detachments in the Four Courts come under attack from troops of the Provisional Government, marking the start of the civil war. The subsequent fighting sees great damage done to the country's infrastructure.

August 30 — Ernest Blythe becomes the Minister in succession to W.T. Cosgrave, who on 25 August became chairman of the Provisional Government in succession to Michael Collins.

September 9 — The third Dáil assembles, minus the anti-treaty group of TDs.

October 25 — The Dáil approves the Constitution of the Irish Free State (Saorstát Éireann).

130

December 6   The Irish Free State comes into existence. The Dáil elects W.T. Cosgrave, President of the Executive Council.

December 21   The Local Elections Postponement Act 1922 marks the first of many occasions on which central government defers holding local elections. (See also June 27, 1973.)

1923

March 28   The Local Government (Temporary Provisions) Act 1923 gives power to dissolve local authorities. It also provides for the validation of county schemes made by county councils during 1921 and 1922 abolishing the workhouse system and the Boards of Guardians, and for the creation of county boards of health.

April 17   The Electoral Act 1923 gives effect to the franchise and electoral provisions of the constitution, and consolidates electoral law.

May 9   The Minister dissolves Kerry County Council, the first local authority to be dissolved in the Irish Free State. Philip Monahan becomes the commissioner.

May 24   Frank Aiken, the IRA chief of staff, issues the ceasefire order which marks the end of the civil war.

May 29   The Minister dissolves Leitrim County Council.

August 8   The Valuation (Postponement of Revision Act) 1923 is the first evidence of the state's enduring unwillingness to grasp the valuation nettle, a failure which culminates in the Supreme Court decision of January 1984 barring the levying of rates on agricultural land. (See also December 7, 1938).

August 27   The general election, the first in Ireland in which every territorial constituency is contested, is held. The results are: Cumann na nGaedheal 63, Sinn Féin 44, Labour 14, Farmers 15, and others 17. Sinn Féin is committed to a policy of abstention from the Dáil.

October 15   Seamus de Burca succeeds Ernest Blythe as the Minister.

November 21   The Minister dissolves Dublin Board of Guardians.

December 28   The Local Authorities (Indemnity) Act 1923 establishes the validity of certain acts done by and omissions made by local authorities between 31 March 1920 and 6 December 1922.

131

1924

March 11   The Minister dissolves New Ross Urban District Council.

April 12   The Local Government (Collection of Rates) Act 1924 enables the Minister to arrange for the collection of rates through the Post Office for a limited period. This was done in counties Kerry and Sligo.

April 21   The Housing (Building Facilities) Act 1924 has as its initial object the revival of private house building. It is extended to urban local authority housing by an amending act of 18 December 1924.

                  The Ministers and Secretaries Act 1924 consolidates central government into eleven departments, including the Department of Local Government and Public Health.

May 20   The Minister dissolves Dublin Corporation.

May 27   The Minister dissolves Kilrush Urban District Council.

July 10   The Dublin Reconstruction (Emergency Provisions) Act 1924 confers wide powers on Dublin Corporation to enable the reconstruction of areas, streets and buildings destroyed or damaged in 1922 during the early months of the civil war.

August 1   The Local Government (Rates on Agricultural Land) Act 1924 gives discretionary powers to county councils to abate up to two-thirds of the rates on agricultural land for the financial year 1924-25. Twelve county councils avail of this measure.

September 4   The Minister dissolves Offaly County Council.

October 22   The Minister dissolves Tipperary Urban District Council.

October 30   The Minister dissolves Cork Corporation. Philip Monahan becomes the commissioner.

October 31   The Minister dissolves Cobh Urban District Council.

1925

March 26   The Local Government Act 1925 abolishes Rural District Councils, centralises public health administration in each county by the creation of Boards of Health and Public Assistance, makes the Minister's power of dissolution of local authorities permanent, empowers county councils to adopt the provisions of the Public Libraries (Ireland) Act 1855, and contains important provisions in regard to roads and the superannuation of officers.

132

April 2	The Police Forces Amalgamation Act 1925 marks the disappearance of the last vestige of local control of/contribution towards policing in Ireland, as the Dublin Metropolitan Police is absorbed into the Garda Síochána.
April 17	The Housing Act 1925 provides for state grants for private and public utility society and local authority housing.
June 23	Local elections are held.
June 27	The Local Authorities (Combined Purchasing) Act 1925 promotes economy in purchasing and a better standard of goods supplied, giving temporary statutory effect to the informal scheme inaugurated by Dáil Éireann in December 1921.
July 11	The Arterial Drainage Act 1925 provides for the formation of new drainage districts, lays down a procedure for dealing with petitions to the county council to have drainage works carried out, and empowers the councils to appoint drainage committees.
July 15	The Local Government (Rates on Agricultural Land) Act 1925 provides for a supplementary agricultural grant by the state in addition to the sum payable under the Local Government (Ireland) Act, 1898 — the first of many such supplementary grants to be made under legislation.
October 28	The Minister dissolves Westport Urban District Council.

1926

April 13	The Street Trading Act 1926 regulates street trading in the County Borough of Dublin and empowers other county borough corporations, borough corporations and urban district councils to adopt the act.
April 14	The Minister dissolves Ennis Urban District Council.
April 18	The first census of population since independence is held.
July 17	The Minister dissolves Trim Urban District Council.
	The Local Authorities (Mutual Assurance) Act 1926 authorises a mutual insurance scheme amongst local authorities.
July 28	The Local Authorities (Officers and Employees) Act 1926 establishes the Local Appointments Commission.
November 29	The report of the Greater Dublin Commission is submitted to the Minister.

1927

June 9	The general election results in continued Cumann na nGaedhael government. Fianna Fáil's decision to enter the Dáil copperfastens the development of democratic politics in independent Ireland.
June 23	Richard Mulcahy succeeds Seamus de Burca as the Minister.
September	The report of the Commission on the Relief of the Sick and Destitute Poor is published.
September 15	The general election results in continued Cumann na nGaedhael government, in coalition with the Farmers Party.
December 10	The Local Elections Act 1927 amends the law relating to local elections.

1928

June	Local elections are held.
June 7	The Local Government (Rates on Small Dwellings) Act 1928 transfers the liability for rates on dwellings of a certain valuation from the occupier to the owner, with a discount for prompt payment.
June 14	The Minister dissolves Bray Urban District Council.
June 15	The Minister dissolves Howth Urban District Council.
July 30	The Local Authorities (Mutual Assurance) Act 1928 gives retrospective protection to the Irish Public Bodies Mutual Insurances Limited established under the 1926 Act.
October 28	The Library Association of Ireland is founded as the professional body for Irish librarians.

1929

February 23	The Cork City Management Act 1929 sets a precedent for the management system throughout Ireland. Philip Monahan is appointed City Manager by name in the Act.
May 14	The Housing Act 1929 makes further provision for state grants for private and local authority housing.
November 7	The Minister dissolves Bundoran Urban District Council.
December 20	The Housing (Gaeltacht) Act 1929 authorises special grants and loans in Irish-speaking areas.

1930

February 26   The National Monuments Act 1930 enables local authorities to appoint national monument advisory committees.

April 15   The State Lands (Workhouses) Act 1930 removes workhouse lands from the operation of the State Lands Act 1924.

July 17   The Local Government (Dublin) Act 1930 brings city management to Dublin and establishes the new corporation of Dun Laoghaire.

July 21   Under the Vocational Education Act 1930 a national vocational education system under local control is introduced.

September 2   The Minister dissolves Kerry County Council.

November 19   The Minister dissolves Galway Board of Health and Public Assistance.

1931

January 1   The Minister dissolves Mayo County Council for rejecting the recommendation of the Local Appointments Commissioners of Ms Letitia Dunbar-Harrison, a Protestant, as County Librarian.

March 29   The Agriculture Act 1931 establishes county committees of agriculture to be appointed and partly funded by county councils, to assist the development of agriculture and of rural industry. (See also June 27, 1988).

April 22   The report of the Commission of Inquiry into De-rating is published.

May 7   Muintir na Tíre is founded in Tipperary town by Reverend John Hayes.

May 27   The Tourist Traffic (Development) Act 1931 empowers local authorities to contribute to an approved tourism company.

July 8   The Local Government Act 1931 strengthens the Minister's powers in relation to dissolved authorities.

December 24   The Housing (Miscellaneous Provisions) Act 1931 provides a more speedy method for the clearance of unhealthy areas and the repair or demolition of houses unfit for human habitation.

1932

February 16	The general election results in the accession to office of a Fianna Fáil minority government under Eamon de Valera.
March 9	Seán T. O'Kelly becomes the Minister.
August 3	The Housing (Financial and Miscellaneous Provisions) Act 1932 repeals the financial provisions of the 1931 Act, increases the state subsidies for local authority housing, increases grants for private housing and simplifies the procedure for the acquisition of land for rural housing.
November 8	The Minister dissolves Wicklow Urban District Council.

1933

January 24	In the general election Fianna Fáil retain power.
April	The Commission of Inquiry into the sale of cottages and plots under the Labourers (Ireland) acts submits its final report. This leads to the eventual enactment of the Labourers Act 1936.
July 27	The Public Hospitals Act 1933 establishes the Hospitals Trust Fund (deriving its income from the Sweepstakes) out of which many new local authority hospitals are built in the ensuing years.

1934

February 20	The Minister dissolves Tipperary (South Riding) County Council.
May 5	The Registration of Maternity Homes Act 1934 provides for the registration and inspection of maternity homes by local authorities.
May 11	The Local Services (Temporary Economies) Act 1934 requires local authorities to make a deduction from the salary of every officer during the financial year 1934/35.
May 29	The Town and Regional Planning Act 1934 enables but does not require councils to adopt development control powers.
June 2	The Minister dissolves Kilkenny County Council.
June 5	The Minister dissolves Laois County Council.

June 6	The Minister dissolves Waterford County Council.
	The Public Assistance (Acquisition of Land) Act 1934 empowers public assistance authorities to acquire land compulsorily. This clears the way for the construction of a number of new county and other hospitals with grants from the Hospitals Trust Fund.
June 26	Local elections are held.
September 6	Under the Limerick City Management Act 1934, Limerick becomes the third city to acquire a management system.
December 21	The Local Government (Amendment) (No.2) Act 1934 provides for the division of a county into two or more county health districts. The measure was availed of only by Cork County Council, which was divided into three county health districts from 1 April 1935.

1935

January 18	The Rates on Agricultural Land (Relief) Act 1935 provides for the application of the relief according to a new formula — primary, employment and supplementary allowances.
February 19	Under the Public Dance Halls Act 1935, local authorities have to be notified of applications for licences to hold public dances. This is an important provision for public health and safety considerations.
March 29	The Local Government (Extension of Franchise) Act 1935 gives local election voting rights to citizens on the same basis as in Dáil elections.
April 17	The Local Loans Fund Act 1935 lays the foundation for the local authority capital finance system for the next fifty-three years. (See also January 1, 1988).
May 24	The Pounds (Provision and Maintenance) Act 1935 requires local authorities to provide and maintain pounds.
	The Courthouses (Provision and Maintenance) Act 1935 updates the law requiring local authorities to provide and maintain courthouses.
June 1	The Minister dissolves Longford Urban District Council.
June 7	The Minister dissolves Westmeath County Council.
June 14	The Milk and Dairies Act 1935 gives sanitary authorities the power to regulate the standard of milk supplied to the public.

August 13	The Minister dissolves Listowel Urban District Council.
December 12	The Slaughter of Animals Act 1935 gives sanitary authorities important powers in relation to the slaughter of animals.

1936

April 26	The census of population takes place.
June 29	The Labourers Act 1936 provides for the purchase by the tenants of cottages provided under the Labourers acts by means of the payment of a terminable annuity.
September 8	The new City Hall in Cork is opened. It replaces the building destroyed in the sack of Cork on 11-12 December 1920.
November 28	The Local Authorities (Miscellaneous Provisions) Act 1936, known as the 'Listowel Act' because of the bizarre administration of Listowel Urban District Council and subsequent court proceedings, amends the law on the borrowing powers of a sanitary authority and limits to one year the time for questioning the validity of local elections.
December 22	James Hurson is appointed secretary of the Department of Local Government and Public Health.

1937

May 5	The Minister dissolves Waterford Corporation.
June 10	The Local Government (Galway) Act 1937 restores borough corporation status and the mayoralty to Galway after a lapse of ninety-seven years.
July 1	A general election and plebiscite on the new draft constitution are held. Fianna Fáil retain office, and the constitution is adopted by the people.
August 26	The Urban Districts (Alteration of Boundaries) Regulations 1937 lay down the procedure on applications by urban district councils for an alteration of their boundaries.
November 19	The Presidental Elections Act 1937 provides a statutory basis for the constitutional provision on the nomination of candidates by county councils and county borough corporations. To date no one has succeeded in obtaining such a nomination.
December 29	Bunreacht na hÉireann comes into effect.

138

1938

March 9	The Minister dissolves Passage West Urban District Council.
June 17	In the General Election, Fianna Fáil retain office.
December 7	The Minister for Finance introduces the Valuation Bill 1938 in the Dáil, proposing a revaluation of every piece of immovable property in the state other than agricultural land and railways. Although it passes the second stage it is not proceeded with owing to the very strong adverse public reaction.
December 20	The Minister dissolves Leitrim Board of Health and Public Assistance.

1939

July 5	The Local Authorities (Combined Purchasing) Act 1939 makes permanent the operation of combined purchasing procedures in existence under the 1925 Act, but this is not brought into operation until 1 January 1961.
July 26	The Air-raid Precautions Act 1939 provides for a civil defence framework based on the local authorities.
July 27	The Rates on Agricultural Land (Relief) Act 1939 is a permanent statute providing rates relief as distinct from the earlier Acts which related to specific years.
August 8	Under the Waterford City management Act 1939 Waterford becomes the fourth city to acquire a manager.
	The Public Assistance Act 1939 abolishes the County Boards of Health and Public Assistance and transfers their functions to county councils, but does not come into operation until 1942.
August 12	The Minister dissolves Buncrana Urban District Council.
September 3	The Emergency Powers Act 1939, under which a number of important orders affecting local authorities are made during the Emergency, comes into operation on the day Britain and France declare war on Germany.
September 8	P.J. Ruttledge becomes the Minister in the government reorganisation which follows the outbreak of World War Two.

139

1940

April 18	The Fire Brigades Act 1940 imposes obligations on sanitary authorities in regard to fires and dangerous buildings.
May 2	The Local Government (Remission of Rates) Act 1940 provides for partial relief of rates in respect of certain new, enlarged and improved residences.
June 13	The County Management Act 1940 introduces county management throughout the country. Some counties are grouped for management purposes. For various reasons the Act does not come into operation until 1942.
June 27	The Local Authorities (Officers and Employees) (Amendment) Act 1940 excludes nurses and midwives from the operation of the 1926 Act.
July 19	The Minister for Supplies announces the appointment of Regional and County Commissioners, with contingent powers and responsibilities, for the duration of the Emergency.
September 4	The Acquisition of Derelict Sites Act 1940 provides for the acquisition of derelict sites by sanitary authorities.
October 11	The Minister dissolves Monaghan Board of Health and Public Assistance.

1941

January 10	The Minister dissolves Granard Urban District Council.
March 21	Owing to the virtual cessation of coal imports, the government empowers local authorities to promote turf production under the Emergency Powers (No. 73) Order 1941.
August 14	Eamon de Valera, already Taoiseach and Minister for External Affairs, briefly becomes the Minister on the resignation of P.J. Ruttledge.
August 18	Seán MacEntee becomes the Minister in succession to Eamon de Valera.
September 23	The Local Government Act 1941 includes important miscellaneous measures on audit and staff. It also gives the Minister power to remove elected members from office without dissolving the authority itself, and it contains important provisions on the constitution and procedure of local authorities.

140

September 26   The Minister dissolves Dublin County Council.

1942

February 24   The Water Supplies Act 1942 gives important powers to local authorities seeking sources for public water supplies.

April 17   The Minister removes from office the members of the Dublin Board of Assistance. It is the first local authority where the members are removed from office under the 1941 Act, as distinct from the authority being dissolved.

April 22   The Minister removes the members of Clare County Council from office.

June 10   The Minister removes the members of the Killarney Urban District Council from office.

June 25   The County Management (Amendment) Act 1942 provides that commissioners of dissolved authorities receive preferential consideration in the initial appointments of County Managers and makes special provision in regard to the management of Clare and Dublin County Councils.

July 20   The Minister removes the members of Kilkenny Corporation from office.

August 19   Local elections are held.

August 26   The Public Assistance Act 1939 and the County Management Act 1940 are brought into operation.

September 9   Passage West Urban District Council is de-urbanised and is replaced by Town Commissioners.

1943

January 20   The County Managers' Association is formed; the name is changed to the County and City Managers' Association on 21 October 1943.

February 23   A fire at St Joseph's Orphanage in Cavan causes the death of thirty five children and one adult. A tribunal of inquiry is appointed on 25 March.

June 22   In the General Election, Fianna Fáil retain power.

December 31   The Local Government (Officers) Regulations 1943 (which come into operation on 1 February 1944) contain many regulations relating to local authority officers.

141

1944

April 1   Granard Urban District Council is de-urbanised and replaced by Town Commissioners.

April 26   The Local Authorities (Education Scholarships) Act 1944 empowers county and county borough councils to award scholarships to secondary, vocational or other approved schools.

May 30   In the General Election, Fianna Fáil retain power.

June 3   The Minister removes the members of Roscommon County Council from office.

1945

March 1   The Arterial Drainage Act 1945, based mainly on the recommendations of the Drainage Commission of 1938-40, requires local authorities to accept responsibility for the cost of maintenance of arterial drainage schemes carried out by the Commissioners of Public Works. (See also January 1, 1987).

March 6   The Tuberculosis (Establishment of Sanitoria) Act 1945 authorises the Minister to establish sanitoria and to transfer these to local authorities when completed.

May 6   The Minister removes the members of Kerry County Council from office.

May 22   The Mental Treatment Act 1945 provides important safeguards against the arbitrary detention of mental patients, and allows the mentally ill to seek treatment voluntarily in district mental hospitals.

June 14   Local elections are held.

August 4   The Local Authorities (Acceptance of Gifts) Act 1945, empowers local authorities to accept gifts. This arose from George Bernard Shaw's wish to give to Carlow Urban District Council property which he had inherited from his mother.

1946

February 7   The Minister publishes the White Paper *Powers and Functions of Elected Members of Local Bodies.*

February 19   The Housing (Amendment) Act 1946 provides for a grant for an extra room for a person suffering from tuberculosis.

142

April 2	The Harbours Act 1946 provides a new legal basis for harbour authorities. Kilrush and Youghal Urban District Councils are the only local authorities which are harbour authorities under the Act.
May 12	The census of population takes place.
June 27	The Finance Act 1946 establishes the Transition Development Fund, out of which grants are made to local authorities for their capital programmes.
August 7	The Local Government Act 1946 includes important provisions on staff, audit, roads, bridges and finance.
August 27	The Labour Court is established under the Industrial Relations Act 1946.
September 30	The Local Government (Officers' Age Limit) Order 1946 fixes the age limit for all pensionable officers of local authorities at 65 years.
November 12	T.J. McArdle is appointed secretary of the Department of Local Government and Public Health.
November 21	The Public Bodies Order 1946 (amended a number of times by subsequent orders) establishes new rules to govern the keeping of accounts and records by local authorities.
December 24	The Ministers and Secretaries (Amendment) Act 1946 provides for the creation of new departments of Health and of Social Welfare.
	During the year the government publishes its seminal White Paper on *Tuberculosis*, outlining an ambitious scheme to tackle the disease.

1947

January 22	The Department of Local Government and Public Health becomes the Department of Local Government. Separate Departments of Health and of Social Welfare are established.
	Dr James Ryan becomes the first Minister for Health.
	T.J. McArdle is appointed the first secretary of the Department of Health.
	John Collins is appointed secretary of the Department of Local Government.
March 18	The Health (Transfer of Departmental Administration and Ministerial Functions) Order 1947 transfers various health functions from the Minister to the Minister for Health.

August 13   The Health Act 1947 increases the health responsibilities of county councils.

September   The White Paper *Outline of Proposals for the Improvement of the Health Services* is published.

September 1   Pádraig Ó Cinnéide is appointed secretary of the Department of Health.

December 10   The Harbours Act 1947 empowers local authorities to give financial assistance to harbour authorities.

December 17   An Chomhairle Leabharlanna is established under the Public Libraries Act 1947.

December 27   The Health Services (Financial Provisions) Act 1947 empowers the Minister for Health to make grants to health authorities.

1948

January   The White Paper *Housing: a Review of Past Operations and Immediate Requirements* is issued.

January 13   The Housing (Amendment) Act 1948 removes the exemption of demesne land from compulsory purchase, on foot of a dispute between Westport Urban District Council and the Marquess of Sligo about the grounds of Westport House. The new measure enables the Urban District Council to build local authority housing at a site near the main entrance to the grounds of Westport House.

January 14   The Local Government (Sanitary Services) Act 1948 gives powers amongst other miscellaneous measures for the prohibition of temporary dwellings.

The Local Government (Superannuation) Act 1948 provides a new superannuation code for local authority officers and employees.

January 30   The County Management (Reserved Functions) Order, 1948, extends the number of reserved functions.

February 4   In the General Election, Fianna Fáil lose office. They are succeeded by a five party 'interparty government' led by John A. Costello of Fine Gael.

February 18   Timothy J. Murphy (Labour) becomes the Minister for Local Government. Dr Noel Browne (Clann na Poblachta) becomes Minister for Health.

144

March 3   The Minister for Health sets up the National Health Council under the Health Act 1947 to advise him on health matters. The council is reconstituted under the Health Act 1953 and given extended terms of reference.

August   The Minister for Health sets up the National Blood Transfusion Association to provide a blood transfusion service. It commmences work in April 1950.

November 11   John Garvin is appointed secretary of the Department of Local Government.

December 1   Tramore Town Commissioners come into being, the first new local authority since the foundation of the state.

1949

May 3   William Norton (Labour) becomes the Minister as a stopgap measure following the sudden death of T.J. Murphy.

May 11   Michael Keyes (Labour) becomes the Minister.

July 20   The Local Authorities (Works) Act 1949 enables local authorities to carry out works for the relief of and for protection against flooding. State grants of 100% are made available for such works.

1950

April 1   The Urban District Councils of Belturbet and Cootehill are de-urbanised and become town commissioners.

June   The Minister for Health arranges for the Medical Research Council to carry out a 'National Tuberculosis Survey'.

June 27   The Local Government (County Administration) Bill 1950 is introduced in the Dáil. It proposes replacing the management system with a system of administration by (a) small executive committees and (b) county officers. The Bill lapses with the dissolution of the Dáil on 7 May 1951.

July 31   The Food Hygiene Regulations 1950 are made to ensure cleanliness in the handling of food.

September 20   Local elections are held.

November 22   The Local Government (Repeal of Enactments) Act 1950 repeals a large number of obsolete laws, dating back as far as 1816, as the first step towards the simplification and modernisation of local government law.

145

December 20	The Industrial Development Authority Act 1950 establishes the Industrial Development Authority.

1951

April 8	The census of population takes place.
April 11	Dr Noel Browne, the Minister for Health, resigns following controversy over his 'mother and child' scheme. The Taoiseach John A. Costello succeeds him as the Minister for Health.
May 8	The Arts Act 1951 establishes the Arts Council.
May 17	The National Mass Radiography Association is incorporated, having begun operating on an informal basis in the previous year. Its purpose is to provide a national mass X-ray service.
May 30	In the general election, the Inter-party government loses power to Fianna Fáil.
June 14	Patrick Smith becomes the Minister. Dr James Ryan again becomes Minister for Health.
October	The White Paper *Reconstruction and Improvement of County Homes* is published. This leads to the modernisation of a number of the old workhouse buildings.

1952

January 22	The Undeveloped Areas Act 1952 establishes An Foras Tionscal to promote industrial development in undeveloped areas.
June 14	The Social Welfare Act 1952 establishes a co-ordinated system of social insurance.
July	The White Paper *Proposals for Improved and Extended Health Services* is published.
July 22	The Housing (Amendment) Act 1952 provides for state grants for private water supplies and sanitation and empowers local authorities to make supplementary grants for such purposes as well as for the erection and reconstruction of houses.
December 3	The Minister removes from office the members of Buncrana Urban District Council for failure to strike a rate following the general revision of valuation of the urban district. Buncrana's grievance over revaluation was resolved by the Local Government (Temporary Reduction of Valuation) Acts of 1954 and 1960 and the Local Government (Buncrana) Act 1968.

1953

Spring

The first issue of *Administration* is published. In 1957 it becomes the quarterly journal of the Institute of Public Administration.

April 1

The Local Government Act 1953 — the so-called 'McQuillan Act' — modifies the requirements for declaring a road to be a public road.

June 18

The Local Elections Act 1953 declares that local elections shall be held in the year 1955 and every five years thereafter.

October 29

The Health Act 1953 provides for a free mother and child service to dependants of all persons insured under the Social Welfare Act 1952.

December 23

The Rates on Agricultural Land (Relief) Act 1953 discontinues the supplementary allowance but the employment allowance is increased.

1954

March 10

The National Development Fund Act 1954 establishes the National Development Fund for a four year period for the purpose of financing development projects of a public character. Substantial road improvement grants are made to local authorities from the fund.

March 11

The Commission on Emigration and Other Population Problems, established in 1948, submits its report to the Minister for Social Welfare.

May 18

The General Election results in Fianna Fáil's loss of power to a coalition headed by John A. Costello of Fine Gael.

June 2

Patrick O'Donnell (Fine Gael) becomes the Minister. T.F. O'Higgins (Fine Gael) becomes Minister for Health.

December 9

The Public Authorities (Judicial Proceedings) Act 1954 repeals the Public Authorities Protection Act 1893, which had limited to six months the time for taking legal actions against public authorities, including local authorities.

1955

May 10

The Local Government Act 1955 includes miscellaneous provisions relating to staff and empowers local authorities to employ traffic wardens at schools and to arrange for the discharge of any of their functions by another local authority.

147

June 9   The Factories Act 1955 consolidates the law in regard to health and safety in factories and gives powers to and imposes duties on sanitary authorities, particularly in relation to fire safety.

June 21   The City and County Management (Amendment) Act 1955 adjusts the balance of power between managers and councillors, most notably in Section 4, which provides a means whereby a council can require a manager to act in a particular way where lawful. The Act followed countrywide consultations with local councillors by the Minister.

June 23-July 1   Local elections are held.

The Law Relating to Local Government by H.A. Street is published during the year.

1956

February 14   The Gaming and Lotteries Act 1956 prohibits gaming in any area unless the local authority adopts Part III of the Act.

March 27   The Local Government (Superannuation) Act 1956 amends the law on the superannuation of officers and employees.

April 8   The census of population is held.

July 25   The Housing (Amendment) Act 1956 provides for the guaranteeing by a housing authority of loans made by a building society.

December 12   The Milk and Dairies (Amendment) Act 1956 updates the 1935 legislation on local authority regulation of milk standards.

1957

March 5   Fianna Fáil under Eamon de Valera regain power in the general election.

March 20   Patrick Smith becomes the Minister. Seán MacEntee becomes the Minister for Health.

November 6   The Institute of Public Administration is founded.

November 27   Neil Blaney becomes the Minister.

1958

February 19   The Office Premises Act 1958 gives local authorities responsibilities in regard to the standards and facilities of office accommodation.

April 22	The Local Government Act 1958 repeals the statutory tenure of office of managers, and effectively sets a retirement age for them. This disposes of an anomaly which had caused some difficulties with the first generation of managers and which resulted in a successful High Court action by Liam Raftis, the then Waterford City Manager.
July 30	The Housing (Amendment) Act 1958 contains miscellaneous provisions relating to grants and other housing matters and makes permanent the Labourers (Ireland) Act 1883 (and amending legislation) which had been on a continuing temporary basis for seventy-five years under the Expiring Laws acts.
August	This month sees the completion of the country's first Group Water Supply Scheme in Old Court, near Manor Kilbride in County Wicklow. The scheme was conceived and promoted by the local curate, Reverend Joseph Collins.
December	*Economic Development* by T.K. Whitaker is published. This has a profound affect on the national approach to economic development.

1959

June 16	Eamon de Valera resigns as Taoiseach and is succeeded by Seán Lemass.
June 20	Pádraig S. Ó Muireadhaigh is appointed secretary of the Department of Health.

1960

April 12	The Health Authorities Act 1960 establishes the Cork, Dublin, Limerick and Waterford Health Authorities.
May	The Minister requests housing authorities to carry out a detailed survey of housing in their areas.
June 23-30	Local elections are held.
July 26	The Local Government Act 1960 enables a county borough corporation to promote or assist the provision of a concert hall, theatre or opera house. This Act arose from the burning down of the Cork opera house on 12 December 1955.
December 13	The National Building Agency Ltd. is established to supplement the local authorities' housing construction programme.

149

December 21   The Local Government (No.2) Act 1960 changes the law in relation to borrowing for capital purposes and the compulsory acquisition of land by local authorities.

December 28   The Health (Fluoridation of Water Supplies) Act 1960 is an important step forward in preventive health care. It leads to a crucial Supreme Court decision on the rights and responsibilities of the community as against the individual.

1961

February 15   The Derelict Sites Act 1961 repeals the 1940 Act and strengthens the powers of local authorities to deal with derelict sites.

April 9   The census of population takes place. It is the first since 1911 not to record a decline in population.

July 29   The Road Traffic Act 1961 enables the Minister to set speed limits for all vehicles and generally updates road traffic law.

August 3   The Health (Corporate Bodies) Act 1961 enables the Minister for Health to establish corporate bodies to provide ancillary health services.

August 11   The Local Authorities (Education Scholarships) Act 1961 provides for a state grant to the local authorities towards the cost of second level and third level scholarships.

August 17   The Civil Liability Act 1961 makes road authorities responsible for damage caused as a result of their failure to maintain adequately a public road (Section 60), but because of its obvious implications this provision of the Act has not been brought into operation.

October   The Institute of Public Administration establishes a distance-education Diploma in Local Administration, the first such programme. From 1984, the Institute offers a BA in Public Administration (Local Government), validated by the National Council for Educational Awards.

October 4   In the general election, Fianna Fáil under Seán Lemass retain office.

1962

August 7   The Rates on Agricultural Land (Relief) Act 1962 restores a supplementary allowance and increases the primary allowance.

August 8   The Local Government (Sanitary Services) Act 1962 contains important advances in sanitary services legislation.

August 10   The Housing (Loans and Grants) Act 1962 consolidates and amends the law relating to grants and loans and is the first step in the simplification and modernisation of the general housing code.

1963

March   The *Report of the Inter-Departmental Committee on the Problems of Small Western Farms* is published leading to the establishment in each of the Western counties of a County Development Team under the chairmanship of the Chief Agricultural Officer of each county committee of agriculture.

March 1   A scheme of conciliation and arbitration for local authority officers comes into operation.

May 20   The Coast Protection Act 1963 enables the Commissioners of Public Works, on the proposal of local authorities, to make and execute coast protection schemes. This proves a most complex procedure, and consequently has very seldom been used.

August 7   The Local Government (Planning and Development) Act 1963 provides a new framework for physical planning and requires local authorities regularly to prepare development plans for their areas.

August 8   The Commission on Itinerancy, set up in 1960, submits its report to the Taoiseach.

                  The second edition of John Collins's *Local Government*, edited by Desmond Roche, is published by the Institute of Public Administration during the year.

1964

March 26   An Foras Forbartha (National Institute for Physical Planning and Research) is established.

July 4   The Registration of Title Act 1964 requires all land acquired by local authorities to be registered in the Land Registry.

July 28   The Local Government (Sanitary Services) Act 1964 gives powers to sanitary authorities to deal with dangerous places and dangerous structures.

October	The Institute of Public Administration sets up a School of Public Administration which, for the next twenty years, provides full-time courses in Public Administration over one academic year for public servants including local authority personnel.
October 1	The 1963 Planning Act comes into operation.
November	The White Paper *Housing Progress and Prospects* is published.
December 2	The Local Government (Repeal of Enactments) Act 1964 repeals a further swathe of obsolete laws.
December 9	The Rates on Agricultural Land (Relief) Act 1964 increases the primary and supplementary allowances.

1965

January 16	The White Paper on *The Restoration of the Irish Language* is published. It makes specific recommendations in respect of local administration.
January 25	The county development teams are reconstituted with the county managers as chairmen.
March 30	The report of the Commission of Inquiry on Mental Handicap is presented to the Minister for Health.
April 1	Kilkenny and Waterford are de-grouped for county management purposes, the first such de-grouping.
April 7	In the general election Fianna Fáil under Seán Lemass retain office.
April 21	Donogh O'Malley becomes the Minister for Health.
May 11	The Mines and Quarries Act 1965 consolidates and amends the law relating to mines and quarries.
May 24	The Minister requests housing authorities to make comprehensive assessments of housing needs for both short and long term building programmes.
July 13	Seán Flanagan becomes the Minister for Health.
October 15	*Valuation for Rating Purposes*, the first report of the Inter-Departmental Committee on Local Finance and Taxation, is published.

1966

| January | The White Paper on *The Health Services and their Further Development* is published. |

152

March 1	The Diseases of Animals Act 1966 consolidates the law relating to diseases of animals but does not materially change the role of the local authorities.
April 17	The census of population takes place.
July	The *Report and Advisory Outline Plan for the Limerick Region* by Professor Nathaniel Lichfield and Associates is submitted to the Minister.
July 12	The Housing Act 1966 repeals more than fifty earlier housing Acts and rationalises housing law.
September 10	Donogh O'Malley, the Minister for Education, announces free post-primary education from September 1967.
October 1	Michael Lawless is appointed secretary of the Department of Local Government.
November 10	Seán Lemass resigns as Taoiseach and is succeeded by Jack Lynch.
November 11	The report of the Commission of Inquiry on Mental Illness is presented to the Minister for Health.
November 16	Kevin Boland becomes the Minister in succession to Neil Blaney.
December	The *Final Report and Advisory Outline Plan for the Dublin Region* by Professor Myles Wright is submitted to the Minister.

1967

March 7	The Industrial Training Act 1967 establishes An Chomhairle Oiliúna (AnCO) as the national industrial and commercial training body.
June 28	Local elections are held
	The Rates on Agricultural Land (Relief) Act 1967 derates the first £20 of holdings under £33 valuation.
August	*Exemptions from and Remissions of Rates,* the second report of the Inter-Departmental Committee, is published.
December 20	The National Rehabilitation Board is established to advise the Minister for Health on all aspects of the rehabilitation of disabled persons and to perform a range of functions on behalf of the Minister.
	Local Government Abroad, volume 4 of the report of the Maud committee on the management of local government in the United Kingdom, is published during the year. It includes a section on the management system in Ireland.

153

1968

February 23   The Limerick, Clare and Tipperary (North Riding) Regional Development Organisation is established on the initiative of the planning authorities in that area — the first such organisation in the state.

March 26   The Local Government (Roads and Drainage) Act 1968 enables county councils to undertake work on non-public roads and minor drainage works and provides for state grants for such works.

June 17   The report of the Consultative Council on the General Hospital Services — the Fitzgerald report on the *Outline of the Future Hospital System* — is published.

July   *Rates and Other Sources of Revenue for Local Authorities*, the third report of the Inter-Departmental Committee, is published.

July 15   The Local Authorities (Higher Education Grants) Act 1968 requires local authorities to administer higher education grants on behalf of the Minister of Education and, following the introduction of free post-primary education, repeals the 1944 and 1961 Acts.

July 16   The Road Traffic Act 1968 provides for local authority traffic wardens to assist the Gardai in operating the 'fine-on-the-spot' system of penalties.

September   *Regional Studies in Ireland* — the 'Buchanan report' — is submitted to the Minister. It is published in May 1969.

November 29   An inter-departmental committee submits a report on *Care of the Aged*. This leads to the establishment of welfare homes by health authorities.

1969

January 1   A Widows and Orphans Contributory Pension Scheme is introduced for local authority officers.

April 1   Tipperary North Riding and Tipperary South Riding are de-grouped for county management purposes.

April 25   The Minister removes from office the members of Dublin Corporation for refusing to strike a rate. John Garvin, lately secretary of the Department of Local Government, is appointed Commissioner.

June   The White Paper *Housing in the Seventies* is published.

June 6   The Minister removes from office the members of Bray Urban District Council.

June 18	In the General Election, Fianna Fáil under Jack Lynch retain power.
July	The Minister appoints a committee to review local authority engineering organisations. This reports in December 1970, and a restructuring of local authority engineering organisations follows.
July 2	Erskine Childers becomes the Minister for Health.
July 15	The Housing Act 1969 controls the demolition or use otherwise than as human habitation of certain houses.
July 25	The Minister requests city and county managers in all regions other than the mid-west to establish Regional Development Organisations.
July 30	The Decimal Currency Act 1969 introduces decimal currency as from 15 February 1971.
September 24	The report of the 'Devlin group' — the Public Services Organisation Review Group 1966-1969 — is published. It includes an important addendum on local government by one of the group, T.J. Barrington.

1970

February 24	The Health Act 1970 establishes eight area health boards to take over local authority functions in health matters.
	The Local Government (Rates) Act 1970 provides for the waiver of rates by rating authorities and for the payment of rates in instalments in certain cases.
May 9	Robert Molloy becomes the Minister in succession to Kevin Boland, who resigns on an issue of Northern Ireland policy.
August	The Minister launches the Guaranteed Order Housing Project.
August 5	The Housing Act 1970 contains a number of miscellaneous housing provisions.
October 1	The Chief Executive Officers of the eight new area health boards take up duty.

1971

February 11	The White Paper on *Local Government Reorganisation* is published.
March	The Minister establishes the Irish Water Safety Association to promote a comprehensive programme of water safety and life-saving. It is made a corporate body on 1 August 1980.

April 1	The eight new area health boards take control of the health services.
April 7	The Local Government Services (Corporate Bodies) Act 1971 enables the Minister to establish corporate bodies to provide services for him and the local authorities.
April 18	The census of population takes place.
May	Comhairle na Gaeilge's report on *Local Government and Development initiatives for the Gaeltacht* is published.
July 13	The Local Government (Rateability of Rents) Act 1971 abolishes the rateability of rents in respect of premises which are exempt from rating.
July 15	The Local Government Staff Negotiations Board is established.
September 1	The Prohibition of Forcible Entry and Occupation Act 1971 prohibits forcible entry and occupation of property. This was enacted to deal with the growing problem of squatting.
October 1	The National Social Service Council is established to advise the Minister for Health on the development of social services generally, including voluntary bodies. It is re-established, under the National Social Service Board Act 1984, as the National Social Service Board.

1972

March 16	*Strengthening the Local Government Service*, a report by McKinsey and Company, Inc., is published.
June 14	The Dangerous Substances Act 1972 consolidates and amends the law relating to explosives, petroleum and other dangerous substances.
July 4	The Local Elections Act 1972 removes certain disqualifications on membership of local authorities.
December	The White Paper on *Local Finance and Taxation* is published.
December 7	In the Referendum to amend the Constitution the proposal to lower the minimum age of voting from 21 to 18 is approved. The Electoral (Amendment) Act 1973 gives effect to this change for local government elections.
December 28	The County Management (Amendment) Act 1972 transfers the power of appointment of county rate collectors from the elected members to the manager, the only local authority appointment that had since 1942 been reserved to the members.

156

1973

January 1	Ireland becomes a member of the European Communities.
February 28	In the general election, Fianna Fáil lose office and are succeeded by a coalition government under Liam Cosgrave of Fine Gael.
March	The Kenny report on the price of building land is submitted to the Minister.
March 14	James Tully (Labour) becomes the Minister.
June 27	The Local Elections Act 1973 empowers the Minister to postpone local elections by Order, subject to confirmation by both houses of the Oireachtas, a simplification of the postponement procedure.
July	The Minister establishes the National Road Safety Association to promote road safety publicity and education. It becomes a corporate body on 8 April 1974.
September	The Minister establishes the Local Government Manpower Committee, a standing advisory body.
November	The National Economic and Social Council is established to provide a forum for discussion of the efficient development of the national economy and the achievement of social justice.
November 21	The Place-Names (Irish Forms) Act 1973 authorises the Minister for Finance by Order to declare the equivalent in the Irish language of a place-name specified in the Order.
December	The Minister issues a discussion document on *Local Government Reorganisation.*
December 24	The Arts Act 1973 enables local authorities to assist the arts.

1974

February 27	The Exchequer and Local Finance Year Act 1974 provides that from 1 January 1975, the local authority financial year shall be the calendar year.
April 2	The Local Government (Roads and Motorways) Act 1974 empowers local authorities to construct motorways. The Naas by-pass is the first motorway constructed under this measure.
May 15	The Local Elections (Petitions and Disqualifications) Act 1974 deals with local election petitions and modifies the restrictions on members of local authorities holding office.

| June 7 | Gerard Meagher is appointed secretary of the Department of Local Government. |
| June 18 | Local elections are held. |

1975

	This year is designated 'European Architectural Heritage Year' by the Council of Europe.
January	Ireland becomes a recipient of allocations from the European Regional Fund. Ireland is treated as a single unit for regional fund purposes, with the Department of Finance in control.
January 1	Carlow and Kildare are de-grouped for county management purposes.
February	The Minister sets up an informal Water Pollution Advisory Council to advise him on the control of water pollution. This is superseded on 13 June 1977 by the Water Pollution Advisory Council appointed under the 1977 Water Pollution Act.
July	The report of the Working Party on the Fire Service is published.
July 12	The Local Authorities (Traffic Wardens) Act 1975 increases the functions of local authorities in relation to the regulation of traffic.
July 15	The EEC issues its Directive on Waste (75/442).
September 17	The Local Government Computer Services Board is established.
December	The Economic and Social Research Institute publishes a report by Brendan Walsh and John Copeland on *Economic Aspects of Local Authority Expenditure and Finance.*
December 8	The EEC issues its Directive on the Quality of Bathing Water (76/160).
December 17	The Social Welfare (Supplementary Welfare Allowance) Act 1975 abolishes home assistance and provides instead for the granting of supplementary welfare allowances by the health boards.

1976

| March 2 | The Rates on Agricultural Land (Relief) Act 1976 discontinues the employment allowance. |

July 5   An Bord Pleanála is established by the Local Government (Planning and Development) Act 1976. The board takes over its appeals function on 15 March 1977.

December 1   Leitrim and Sligo are de-grouped for county management purposes.

1977

March 15   The Local Government (Water Pollution) Act 1977 provides local authorities with increased powers and responsibilities to control water pollution.

June 1   Longford and Westmeath are de-grouped for county management purposes.

June 16   In the general election, the Cosgrave coalition loses to Fianna Fáil.

July 5   Sylvester Barrett becomes the Minister.

August 16   The Department of Local Government becomes the Department of the Environment.

November 11   The Minister issues the Superannuation Revision Scheme 1977 to local authorities.

1978

June   The Minister sets up a three-year Environmental Council to advise him on environmental matters.

July 5   The Finance Act 1978 winds up the Road Fund established under the Roads Act 1920. All future road grants are paid out of exchequer funds.

July 20   The Minister establishes the Fire Prevention Council to promote greater public awareness of fire hazards.

December 20   The Local Government (Financial Provisions) Act 1978 gives full relief of rates, as from 1 January 1978, to domestic dwellings and some other properties on the basis of full recoupment to the local authority by the exchequer, and gives the Minister power to limit rate increases on the remaining rateable properties. This measure accomplishes the removal of domestic rates, an end to which both the major political parties had been committed for some time.

1979

January 8	A fire on the oil tanker *Betelgeuse* at Whiddy Island Oil Terminal causes fifty deaths. A Tribunal of Inquiry established on 8 March 1979 submits its report to the Minister for Transport on 9 May 1980.
April 1	The census of population is taken.
May	The *Road Development Plan for the 1980s* is published by the Government.
June	Co-operation North is founded.
June 7	Local elections are held.
July/Iuil	Bhunaigh an tAire Grúpa Stiúrtha le h-úsáid na Gaeilge go toilteanach a spreagadh sa tseirbhís rialtais áitiúil.
August 1	The Housing (Miscellaneous Provisions) Act 1979 enables the Minister to devolve the administration of housing grants to housing authorities and validates the changes in grants, loans and subsidies made since 1972.
December 12	The Local Government (Toll Roads) Act 1979 gives power to charge tolls on specified roads. The first toll bridge, the East Link bridge in Dublin, is opened in October 1984.
	Jack Lynch resigns as Taoiseach and is succeeded by Charles J. Haughey.

1980

January	The Minister asks housing authorities to carry out an assessment of actual and prospective housing needs.
January 1	Údarás na Gaeltachta is established under the Údarás na Gaeltachta Act 1979 to promote economic and social development in Gaeltacht regions. The authority includes directly elected members.
June 4	The Local Government (Superannuation) Act 1980 enables the Minister to make superannuation schemes and repeals the Acts of 1948 and 1956, allowing greater flexibility in formulating superannuation provisions.
June 9	The Safety in Industry Act 1980 updates the Factories Act 1955.
July 1	The Rates on Agricultural Land (Relief) Act 1980 lowers the ceiling of entitlement to relief.

160

July 14	The Ombudsman Act 1980 provides for the appointment of an ombudsman. Local authorities are brought within his ambit from 1 April 1985.
October 15	Ray Burke becomes the Minister.
December 24	The Casual Trading Act 1980 up-dates the law on casual trading.

1981

February 14	A fire at the Stardust Club in Artane, Dublin, causes forty-eight deaths. A Tribunal of Inquiry is appointed to inquire into the tragedy. It reports to the Minister on 30 June 1982, concluding that the fire was probably started deliberately.
February 24	The Social Welfare (Consolidation) Act 1981 consolidates social welfare law.
March 31	The Minister publishes Revised Draft Building Regulations, which are intended to provide a national code of building standards.
April 5	The census of population takes place.
May 6	The Malicious Injuries Act 1981 provides a new code for dealing with malicious injury claims, giving a role to the District Court and empowering local authorities to settle claims.
June 11	In the general election Fianna Fáil lose power to a Fine Gael/Labour coalition headed by Garret FitzGerald
June 30	Peter Barry (Fine Gael) becomes the Minister.
December 16	The Fire Services Act 1981 repeals the 1940 Act and updates and strengthens the law relating to the fire service.
December 27	The Housing Finance Agency Act 1981 provides for the establishment of the Housing Finance Agency for the purposes of raising extra funds for house purchase loans on a self-financing basis.

1982

January 1	Shannon Town Commissioners are established, reflecting the growth of the new town of Shannon.
February 18	In the General Election the FitzGerald coalition loses power to a minority Fianna Fáil administration under Charles J. Haughey.

161

March 1	The Youth Employment Agency is established under the Youth Employment Agency Act 1981.
March 9	Ray Burke again becomes the Minister.
April 1	Laois and Offaly, the remaining such group, are de-grouped for county management purposes.
June 30	The Litter Act 1982 radically strengthens the powers of local authorities to control litter.
July 28	The Local Government (Planning and Development) Act 1982 limits the duration of planning permissions and provides for the payment of fees for planning applications.
October	The Government publishes its national economic plan *The Way Forward 1983-1987.*
November 24	In the general election Fianna Fáil lose office to a Fine Gael/Labour coalition, again led by Garret FitzGerald.
December 14	Dick Spring (Labour) becomes the Minister.
	Local Government in Ireland by Desmond Roche is published by the Institute of Public Administration during the year.

1983

January 1	Following the High Court decision of July 1982 (upheld by the Supreme Court in January 1984) that the valuation system as it operates for agricultural land is repugnant to the Constitution, full rates relief is provided for all land for 1983 and subsequent years.
February	The Travelling People Review Group, set up jointly by the Minister and the Minister for Health in January 1981, submits its report.
March 3	The Local Authorities (Officers and Employees) Act 1983 enables the Local Appointments Commission to resume the practice of awarding credit for knowledge of Irish, which had been discontinued following a High Court decision.
March 28	The Minister opens a new national computerised Vehicle Registration Unit at Shannon.
April 1	Daniel Turpin is appointed secretary of the Department of the Environment.
April 18	Philip Monahan, the first manager, dies in Cork, aged eighty-nine.

May 11	The Local Government (Financial Provisions) Act 1983 clarifies the law in relation to the timing of the making of rates by local authorities.
June 22	The Fire Services Council is established by the Minister under the Fire Services Act 1981 to perform specified functions on behalf of the Minister and fire authorities.
June 30	The Commission of Inquiry on Safety, Health and Welfare at Work submits its report to the Minister for Labour.
July 12	The Local Government (Financial Provisions) (No.2) Act 1983 enables local authorities to charge for services.
July 20	The Local Government (Planning and Development) Act 1983 provides for the reconstitution of An Bord Pleanála.
December 14	Liam Kavanagh (Labour) becomes the Minister.

1984

January 1	Greystones Town Commissioners are established.
January 20	The Supreme Court delivers its long anticipated judgement that the system of assessing agricultural rates is unconstitutional.
February 7	The Housing Act 1984, introduced following a Supreme Court judgement, enables housing authorities to rehouse persons not resident in their functional areas.
March 30	The Social Welfare Act 1984 abolishes local old age pension committees which county councils and certain urban authorities had been entitled to appoint since 1908. Their abolition comes into effect on 2 July 1984.
October	The Government publishes its national plan *Building on Reality 1985-1987.*
October 2	The Minister introduces a grant of £5,000 for local authority tenants of at least three years' standing and local authority tenant purchasers who buy a new or existing private house and surrender their local authority dwelling to the local authority.
October 21	Ireland's first toll bridge for motorists, the East Link bridge spanning the Liffey, is opened. After a number of years in operation in private hands, it will become the property of Dublin Corporation.
December	A career break scheme is introduced for local authority officers.

1985

January	A new roads plan, *Policy and Planning Framework for Roads*, is published.
April 3	The Local Government (Reorganisation) Act 1985 provides for the reorganisation of local government in Dublin County (although this was not put into effect) and for the constitution of Galway Borough as a county borough.
May	The National Economic and Social Council publishes its report on *The Financing of Local Authorities*. The *Fourth Report (Special Taxation) of the Commission on Taxation* is published.
May 30	The Minister issues a policy statement, *The Reform of Local Government*.
June	The Oireachtas Joint Committee on Building Land, established in March 1983, publishes its final report.
June 20	Local elections take place.
June 25	Thomas Troy is appointed secretary of the Department of the Environment.
July 25	The Farm Tax Act 1985 provides for a farm tax on certain agricultural land to be levied and collected by the local authorities. This tax is subsequently abolished from 1 January 1987.
August 2	The members of Naas Urban District Council are removed from office.

1986

	The year is designated European Road Safety Year by the EEC Transport Council.
January 1	Galway becomes a county borough.
February 14	John Boland (Fine Gael) becomes the Minister.
March 4	The Valuation Act 1988 enables fixed plant and constructions other than buildings to be valued.
April 13	The census of population takes place.
May 18	The National Archives Act 1986 provides for the establishing of the National Archives and covers local authority records in the possession of the National Archives.
June 12	The Dublin Transport Authority Act 1986 establishes a new co-ordinating body to develop and implement an urban transportation strategy for the capital.

164

June 24   The Urban Renewal Act 1986 provides for the renewal of designated urban areas.

July 15   The Malicious Injuries (Amendment) Act 1986 provides inter alia that the Minister shall refund the cost of claims to the local authorities.

The National Lottery Act 1986 provides for a national lottery out of which many local authority projects are funded.

December 17   The Control of Dogs Act 1986 consolidates and amends the law relating to the control of dogs and assigns responsibility to the local authorities for its implementation.

December 22   The Electoral (Amendment) (No.2) Act 1986 enables disabled electors to vote at home.

1987

January 1   The Minister introduces a new motor registration system based on the year of first registration and the county of registration.

Responsibility for the cost of maintenance of arterial drainage schemes carried out under the Arterial Drainage Act 1945 is transferred from local authorities to the exchequer.

February 11   The *Report of the Public Library Service Review Group* is published.

February 17   In the general election the FitzGerald coalition loses power to Fianna Fáil under Charles J. Haughey.

March 10   Padraig Flynn becomes the Minister.

March 21   The European Year of the Environment begins. It will run to 20 March, 1988.

June 10   The Air Pollution Act 1987 establishes a legal framework within which relevant European Community requirements can be implemented.

July 1   The Single European Act of the European Community comes into force.

September   The Government decides to abolish the Regional Development Organisations with effect from 1 January 1988.

December 27   The Dublin Transport Authority (Dissolution) Act 1987 removes the body established in the previous year.

1988

January 1   The system of loans for local authority capital projects established under the Local Loans Fund Act 1935 is replaced by a system of capital grants from the exchequer.

The National Safety Council is established by the Minister. It replaces the National Road Safety Association, the Fire Prevention Council and the Irish Water Safety Association which are abolished.

An Foras Áiseanna Saothair (FÁS) is established under the Labour Services Act 1987 as the national training and employment authority. It replaces AnCO, the Youth Employment Agency, and the National Manpower Service of the Department of Labour.

February 8   The Housing Finance Agency (Amendment) Act 1988 enables the agency to lend funds to a housing authority for the making of improvement loans and the payment of supplementary grants.

March 3   The Valuation Act 1988 establishes a Valuation Tribunal to decide valuation appeals.

April 3   The Abattoirs Act 1988 updates and strengthens the law in regard to the slaughter of animals.

June 27   The Agriculture (Research, Training and Advice) Act 1988 dissolves the county committees of agriculture established by the Agriculture Act 1931. The dissolution comes into effect on 8 September, 1988.

July 1   Leixlip Town Commissioners are established.

July 13   The Data Protection Act 1988 gives effect to the Council of Europe Convention of 28 January 1981. Local authorities are bound by the Act.

The Housing Act 1988 empowers housing authorities to provide sites for travellers and contains provisions on the accommodation of the homeless.

July 19   The Local Government (Multi-Storey Buildings) Act 1988 assigns duties to local authorities in regard to buildings of five or more storeys. This arose from investigations into the Raglan House collapse in which two people died.

July 20   The Minister sets up a National Roads Authority on a non-statutory basis.

| September 5 | The Minister establishes the Environmental Research Unit partially to replace An Foras Forbartha, which was abolished on grounds of economy and rationalisation. |
| | The Taoiseach establishes the National Heritage Council. |

1989

| April 19 | The Safety, Health and Welfare at Work Act 1989 establishes the National Authority for Occupational Safety and Health. |
| June 15 | In the general election Fianna Fáil suffer a small loss in seats. The party continues in office under Charles J. Haughey by forming a coalition government with the Progressive Democrats. |

1990

March 21	The Building Control Act 1990 enables the Minister to make building regulations and building control regulations and gives enforcement powers to certain local authorities.
April	The Government establishes sub-regional review committees to assist in monitoring the implementation of European Community Structural Fund measures. These committees include the chairmen of county councils and the managers.
June	The Government appoints an Advisory Expert Committee on Local Government Reorganisation and Reform under the chairmanship of Dr T.J. Barrington.
June 10	The Local Government (Planning and Development) Act 1990 amends the law in regard to claims for compensation under the Planning Acts.
June 25	Brendan O'Donoghue is appointed secretary of the Department of the Environment.
June 27	The Derelict Sites Act 1990 repeals the 1961 Act and strengthens the powers of local authorities to deal with derelict sites, including a derelict site levy in respect of urban land.
July 18	The Local Government (Water Pollution) (Amendment) Act 1990 extends the powers of local authorities to deal with water pollution.
September 26	The Minister launches a new environmental information service (ENFO) in Dublin.

Compilation of this chronology ceased on 31 October 1990.

VII
A BIBLIOGRAPHY OF
LOCAL GOVERNMENT

Maureen Conroy

This bibliography supplements the bibliography in Desmond Roche *Local Government in Ireland* — the definitive study of local government — by listing relevant works published since the publication of that book in 1982. Taken together, they complement the chronology included in this volume as a resource for scholars of local government.

ADVISORY COMMITTEE ON MANAGEMENT TRAINING, *Managers for Ireland: The case for the development of Irish managers,* (Chairperson: E.P. Galvin), Dublin: 50 1988.

AHERN, M.G., 'The evolution of the Limerick, Clare and Tipperary (NR) Regional Development Organisation', *The Engineers Journal,* 35,7/8, July/August 1982, 9-10.

ALMY, T.A., 'The development and evolution of city-county management in Ireland. An illustration of central-local administrative relationships', *International Journal of Public Administration,* 2,4, 1980, 477-500.

BANNON, M.J., 'The changing context of developmental planning', *Administration,* 31, 2, 1983, 112-146.

BANNON, M.J., 'How regionalism could aid the country', *Irish Times,* 5 January 1985, 16.

BANNON, M.J., NOWLAN, K.J., MAWHINNEY, K. and HENDRY, J., *Planning — the Irish experience 1920-1988,* Dublin: Wolfhound Press, 1989, 200 (Bib.).

BARRETT, S., *Transport policy in Ireland,* Dublin: IMI 1982 (Bib.).

BARRINGTON, T.J., 'A ghastly failure but will we learn?', *Irish Times,* 7 January 1985, 2.

BARRINGTON, T.J., *'One person one vote'* (a series of 3 articles) 'Political inequality in local government' Page 11; 'Giving political equality to the counties' page 13; 'A new network of town-rural districts' page 13, *Irish Times,* 18,19 and 20 June 1985.

BARRY, M.A., 'Infrastructure in the south east region', *The Engineers Journal,* 35, 5 May 1982, 7-11.

BENNETT, D., 'Community control of crime', *Social Studies,* 7, 2, Autumn/Winter 1983, 248-260.

BENOIT, P., 'Allocation of powers to the local and regional levels of government in the member states of the Council of Europe', In *Local and regional authorities in Europe,* Strasbourg: Council of Europe study series 42, 1988.

BLACKWELL, John, 'Housing finance in Ireland in the 1980s', *Irish Banking Review,* December 1984, 69-84.

BLACKWELL, John, *Housing requirements and population change 1981-1991,* Dublin: NESC Report 69 (Pl 1110) May 1983.

BLACKWELL, John, 'Paying for housing: policy options', *Administration* Special Issue 36, 4, 1988, 121-135.

BLACKWELL, John, *Population and labour force projections by county and region 1979-1991,* Dublin: NESC Report 63 (Pl 896) July 1982.

BLACKWELL, John, *A review of housing policy,* Dublin: NESC Report, 87 (Pl 6080) December 1988.

BLACKWELL, John, *Some issues in housing policy,* Dublin: UCD Resource and Environmental Policy Centre WP 35, 1986 (Bib.).

BLACKWELL, John and CONVERY, F., *Replace or retain: Irish policies for buildings analysed,* Dublin: UCD Resource and Environmental Policy Centre 1989.

BLACKWELL, John and BRANGAN, E., *Survey of the housing stock 1980: a summary report,* Dublin: Foras Forbartha 1984.

BLACKWELL, John and VAN DER KEMP, H., *The development control system: A survey of the process,* Dublin: Foras Forbartha 1987.

BLACKWELL, John and VAN DER KEMP, H., *The planning laws: A time for change? planning control legislation in practice.* A paper presented to the IPA/LAMA conference held in Galway 24/25 April 1987, Dublin: IPA Library Information File.

BLACKWELL, John and VAN DER KEMP, H., *Regional planning in the 1990s. Review of the planning system,* Dublin: Foras Forbartha, Discussion Paper 1, 1987 (Bib.).

BOYLAN, T.A., 'Industrial development in the west region: achievements and prospects', *The Engineers Journal* 39, 7/8 July/August 1986, 13-16.

BOYLAN, T.A. and CUDDY, M.P., 'Regional industrial policy: performance and challenge', *Administration* 32, 3, 1984, 255-270.

BOYLE, O., *Waste disposal in Ireland: a discussion of the major issues,* Dublin: Foras Forbartha 1987 (Bib.).

BRADY, SHIPMAN and MARTIN, *Development Strategy to 2004: Galway-Mayo region.* A study prepared for the West RDO and the CEC (4 vols) Dublin: Brady, Shipman and Martin 1984.

BRADY, SHIPMAN and MARTIN, *Donegal-Leitrim-Sligo: regional strategy,* Dublin: Brady, Shipman and Martin 1986.

BRANGAN, E. and MULVIHILL, R., *The development control system,* Dublin: DOE Environmental Research Unit 1989.

BRENNAN, B., 'Construction maintenance and management of public housing', *Administration* Special Issue 36, 4, 1988, 88-96.

BRENNAN, S. and MURPHY, C. (eds), *Brennan's key to local authorities,* Dublin: Landscape Press, 1986.

BRESNIHAN, V., 'A community success story: Connemara West', *Studies,* 79, 313, Spring 1990, 63-68.

BUSINESS AND FINANCE, 'Cork holds key to council peace', 28 August 1986, 29; 'Spendthrift councils a threat to democracy', 12 March 1981, 9-10, 12-13.

BUSINESS AND FINANCE SUPPLEMENT, 'The cost of running Cork: an interview with the city manager Joe McHugh', 22 April 1982, 6-7.

BYRNE, P., 'A future for urban authorities', *L.A.N. (Nestron),* 2, 1, 1988,15-.

BYRNE, R., 'Legal aspects of pollution', [for local authorities], *L.A.N. (Nestron),* 4, 4, 1990, 27-.

BYRNE, R. and BINCHY, W., *Annual review of Irish law,* Dublin: Round Hall Press 1982-.

BYRNE, R. and McCUTCHEON, P., *The Irish legal system : cases and materials,* Abingdon, Oxford : Professional Books 1986.

CABOT, D., *EEC environmental legislation : A handbook for local authorities,* Dublin: Foras Forbartha 1986.

CAHILL, C., *Handbook of Irish case law,* Dublin: Round Hall Press 1984.

CASEY, S., 'Role perception among county councillors', *Administration,* 34, 3, 1986, 302-316.

CASEY, T.A., 'Local Government (Water Pollution) Act 1977: the Kerry experience', *The Engineers Journal,* 37, 8, August 1983, 33-34.

CASEY, T.J., *Discussion on planning in local government: A civil engineering viewpoint.* A lecture to the annual conference of the County and City Engineers' Association held in Kinsale 29 October 1985, Dublin: IPA Library Information file.

CENTRAL STATISTICS OFFICE, *Census of Population 1986,* Local reports by county 1-31, Dublin : SO 1987-1988.

CHANDLER, J.A. and LAWLESS, P., *Local authorities and the creation of employment,* Aldershot: Gower 1985 (Bib.).

CHUBB, B., *The government and politics of Ireland,* (2nd Ed.) London: Longman 1982.

COLLERAN, E., *Perspectives on planning,* Paper presented to the IPA/LAMA conference held in Galway, 24/25 April 1987, Dublin: IPA Library Information File.

COLLINS, C.A., 'Clientelism and careerism in Irish local government: The persecution of civil servants revisited', *Economic and Social Review* , 16, 4, July 1985, 273- 286.

COLLINS, N., 'Councillor/officer relations in Irish local government: alternative models', *Public Administration*, 63, 3, Autumn 1985, 327-344.

COLLINS, N., *Local government managers at work: the city and council manager system of local government in the Republic of Ireland*, Dublin: IPA 1987 (Bib.).

COLLINS, N., 'The 1985 local government elections in the Republic of Ireland', *Irish Political Studies*, 1, 1986, 97-102.

COLLINS, N., 'Regional planning structures under the national development plan for the Republic of Ireland', *Irish Political Studies*, 4, 1989, 115-118.

COMMINS, P., 'Rural community development: approaches and issues', *Social Studies*, 8, 3/4 Spring/Autumn 1985, 165-178.

COMMISSION OF THE EUROPEAN COMMUNITIES, *Co-operation in the field of employment initiatives*. Report on a second series of local consultations held in European countries 1984-1985. Luxembourg : Office for Official Publications of the European Communities 1986.

CONNOLLY, D., 'North-east (Roscommon) regional water supply scheme — a report', *L.A.N. (Nestron)*, 1, 1, 1987, 39—.

CONNOLLY, D., 'Roads policy in Ireland — A critical review — A local perspective', *L.A.N. (Nestron)*, 2, 3, 1988, 27-.

CONNOLLY, M., *Central-local government relations in Northern Ireland: the future role and organisation of local government*, Birmingham: University of Birmingham Institute of Local Government Studies, Study Paper, 5, 1986 (Bib.).

CONROY, D., 'Dublin in the rare new times (changing population movements, housing patterns, new roads and infrastructure)', *Business and Finance*, 1 August, 1985, 15.

CONROY, D., 'Nice idea — but will it work? (the Metropolitan Streets Commission in Dublin)', *Business and Finance*, 10 July, 1986, 33-34.

CONROY, D., 'Urban renewal — who will invest?', *Business and Finance*, 25 September 1986, 22-23.

CONVERY, F., 'The physical environment', *Administration*, 30, 2/3, 1982, 243-265.

CONVERY, F., 'Revitalizing Dublin', *Studies*, 77, 306 Summer 1988, 154-164.

CONVERY, F. and SCHMID, A.A., *Policy aspects of land-use planning in Ireland*, Dublin: ESRI Broadsheet Series 22, December 1983.

COONEY, T.A.M., 'An aspect of planning appeal procedures', *Irish Jurist*, xvii NS 1982, 346-351.

COOPER, M., 'Merrell Dow — a test case for chemical investment and how the [Cork] council monitors the effluent', *Business and Finance*, 1 December 1988, 10-14.

CORCORAN, T., 'Government policies towards public housing', *Administration* Special Issue, 36, 4, 1988, 41-51.

COUNCIL OF EUROPE, *European charter of local self government*, Strasbourg: Council of Europe Treaty Series 122, October 1985.

COUNCIL OF EUROPE, *Local authority accounting in Europe*, [including Ireland], Strasbourg: Council of Europe 1985.

COUNCIL OF EUROPE, *Sixth conference of European ministers responsible for local government* held in Rome, 6-8 November 1984 (Conclusions), Strasbourg: Council of Europe 1985.

COUNTY AND COUNTY BOROUGH ELECTORAL AREA, BOUNDARIES COMMISSION, *Report of the commission*, (Chairperson: Ms. Justice O'Carroll), Dublin: SO (PI 3036) 1985.

CRIBBEN, E., 'Dublin corporation housing — A wide ranging strategy', *L.A.N. (Nestron)*, 4, 4, 1990, 3-.

CUDDY, M.P. and BOYLAN, T.A. (Eds), *The future of regional policy in the European Communities: its implications for Ireland*, UCG Social Sciences Centre 1987 (Bib.).

DALY, J.P., 'Local authority waste water treatment plants 1977-1987', *The Engineers Journal*, 41, 1/2 January/February 1988, 28-30.

DEMPSEY, J.R., 'Administrative Reorganisation in Irish and American contexts', *Administration*, 30, 1, 1982, 64-83.

[Development Plans of Local Authorities], 1982-.

DILLON, N., 'Wexford Corporation wins Europa Nostra award', *L.A.N. (Nestron)*, 4, 4, 1990, 33-.

DOE, *Annual reports*, Dublin : SO 1982-.

> *Environment Bulletin*, Quarterly review of developments in the area of environmental protection, Dublin: DOE July/September 1987-.

> *Financing of housing — Ireland 1985*, A monograph prepared for the UN/ECE, Dublin: DOE 1985.

> *Ireland: road development 1989-1993*, Operational programme submitted to the CEC 30 March 1989, Dublin: SO (PI 6482) 1989.

> *Local authority estimates (annual)*, Dublin : SO 1982-.

> *Policy and planning framework for roads*, Dublin: SO (PI 2948) 1985-.

> *Quarterly Bulletin of housing statistics*, Dublin: SO 1982-.

> *The reform of local government*, a policy statement by Liam Kavanagh, Dublin : SO (PI 3228) 1985.

> *Urban development plans for the 1980s*, Guidelines for the preparation of statutory development plans, Dublin: DOE 1983.

> *Urban renewal financial incentives*, Dublin DOE 1986.

DOE ENVIRONMENTAL RESEARCH UNIT, *Dublin Bay water quality: developing a water quality management plan*, Dublin: DOE/ERU 1989.

DEPARTMENT OF FINANCE, *An outline of government contracts procedures*, (PI 4120), Dublin: SO 1986.

DEPARTMENT OF TRANSPORT, *Transport policy: a green paper*, (PI 3580), Dublin : SO 1985.

DONNELLY, P.J., *The council/manager system*, Background notes for the regional seminar for newly elected representatives held in Kilkenny city 9 November 1985 Dublin: IPA Library Information File.

DONOGHUE, D. 'Implications of removal of domestic rates for local government', *Seirbhis Phoibli*, 6, 1, January 1985, 35-37.

DOODY, M., 'Waterford designated area — exciting changes for Waterford', *L.A.N. (Nestron)*, 3, 1, 1989, 20-.

DOYLE, G.M., 'Community policing', *Social Studies*, 7, 2, Spring 1983, 43-158.

DUBLIN CORPORATION, *Inner city development : new incentives for designated areas*, Dublin: Dublin Corporation 1987.

DUBLIN CORPORATION, *Monthly Environmental Health Bulletin*, Dublin: EHOA 1982.

DUBLIN ELECTORAL AREA BOUNDARIES COMMISSION, *Report of the Commission*, Dublin: SO (PI 3035) 1985.

DUN LAOGHAIRE HARBOUR PLANNING REVIEW GROUP AND DEPARTMENT OF THE MARINE, *Dun Laoghaire Harbour: Report of the Planning Review Group*, (Chairperson: Dermot McAleese) Dublin: SO 1988 (Bib.).

EASTERN REGIONAL DEVELOPMENT ORGANISATION, *Eastern region settlement strategy 2011*, Main Report and Summary Report, Dublin: ERDO 1985.

ECONOMIC AND SOCIAL RESEARCH INSTITUTE, *Quarterly Economic Commentary*, Dublin: ESRI, 1982-.

ENVIRONMENTAL HEALTH OFFICERS ASSOCIATION, *The Environmentalist*, Quarterly Journal of the EHOA, Dublin: EHOA 1982-.

THE ENVIRONMENTALIST, 'Local Government (Planning and Development) Act 1963-1976: Monaghan County Council v. Brendan Brogan and Patrick Brogan', *The Environmentalist*, 11, 1 Autumn 1988, 6-9.

EUROPEAN FOUNDATION FOR THE IMPROVEMENT OF LIVING AND WORKING CONDITIONS, *Locally-based responses to long-term unemployment* [including Ireland], Luxembourg: Office for Official Publications of the European Communities 1988 (Bib.).

EUROPEAN FOUNDATION FOR THE IMPROVEMENT OF LIVING AND WORKING CONDITIONS, *Taking action about long term unemployment in Europe: the experience of 20 locally-based projects*, Luxembourg: Office for Official Publication of the European Communities 1987.

EUROPEAN INDUSTRIAL RELATIONS REVIEW, 'Code of practice in security of employment for employee grades in local authorities (agreed November 1985)' *European Industrial Relations Review*, 148, May 1986, 25-26.

FARRELL, P., 'New Bill proposes air quality controls (implications for local authorities of the 1986 Air Pollution Bill)', *L.A.N.(IPA)*, Spring 1987, 5.

FEENEY, B.P., 'Paying for road damage', *Promise and performance: Irish environmental policies analysed*, edited by J. Blackwell and F.Convery, Dublin: UCD Resource and Environmental Policy Centre 1983, 367-375.

FEENEY, B.P., *Road infrastructure investment*, Dublin: Foras Forbartha 1982 (Bib.).

FEENEY, B.P. and DEVLIN, J., 'Developing an economic evaluation procedure for road investments', *Irish Journal of Environmental Science* 4, 2, 1987, 1-9 (Bib.).

FIANNA FÁIL, *Power back to the people — the Fianna Fáil alternative: local elections '85*, Dublin: Fianna Fáil 1985.

FINE GAEL, *Living in Dublin: policy proposals*, Dublin: Fine Gael 1988.

FITZGERALD, E., ' A housing policy for today's needs', *Administration* Special Issue 36, 4, 1988, 77-87.

FLEMING, T., 'Infrastructure in the greater Cork area in the nineties', *The Engineers Journal* 42, 6/7, June/July 1989, 27, 29-31.

FLOOD, P. and EISING, J., 'Bridge and road network developments in the Galway area', *The Engineers Journal* 39, 7/8, July/August 1986, 21-23.

FOLEY, A., *Designation of areas for industrial policy*, Dublin: NESC Report 81 (PI 3386) September 1985.

FORAS FORBARTHA, *Abstracts of reports prepared by the Roads Division, Foras Forbartha*, Dublin: 1987.

FORAS FORBARTHA, *The demand for retail space*, (Development plan manual 3) Dublin: 1984.

FORAS FORBARTHA, *EEC Directive on enviromental impact assessment: proceedings of a seminar*, Dublin: 1986.

FORAS FORBARTHA, *Ireland in the year 2000*: a series of colloquies. 'Infrastructure: organisation, finance and employment', 'Towards a national strategy', 'Strategies for employment', 'Urbanisation'. Dublin: 1982-1985.

FORAS FORBARTHA, *Land Use Budgeting* (Development Plan Manual 7). Dublin: 1984.

FOSTER, C. JACKMAN, R. and THOMPSON, A., *The financing of local authorities*, Dublin: NESC Report 80 (PI 3152) May 1985.

GALLAGHER, M., ' Local elections and electoral behaviour in the Republic of Ireland', *Irish Political Studies* 4, 1989, 21-42.

GARDINER, F.K., 'Community security: the Irish problem', *Economic and Social Review* 18, 1, October 1986, 1-15.

GENERAL COUNCIL OF COUNTY COUNCILS, *Tourism in the Irish economy and the role of local authorities*. Eleventh annual conference of the General Council of County Councils held at Ballybunion 18/20 June 1987, Dublin: IPA Information File.

GILLMAN, D.A., 'Village change', *Social Studies* 9, 1/2 Spring/Summer 1986, 56-68.

GOULD, F. and ZARKESH, P., 'Local government expenditures and revenues in Western democracies 1960-1982', [14 countries including Ireland], *Local Government Studies* 12, January/February 1986, 33-42.

GRIMES, R.H. and HORGAN, P.T., *Introduction to law in the Republic of Ireland: its history, principles, administration and substance*, Dublin: Wolfhound Press 1988 (Bib.).

GRIST, B., *Preparation of development plans. A survey of the process.* Dublin: Foras Forbartha 1984.

GRIST, B., *Twenty years of planning. A review of the system since 1963*, Dublin: Foras Forbartha 1983.

GUBBINS, M., 'Wrestling with the deficit [in Cork City]', *Business and Finance* Special Supplement, 21 April 1983, 5, 7.

HARLOFF, C.M., *The structure of local government in Europe: surveys of 29 countries* [including Ireland], The Hague: IULA Publication 1414, 1987 (Bib.).

HART, J., 'Local authorities charge ahead (the options for charging for services)', Autumn 1987,1. LAN(IPA).

HARVEY, S., 'The local enterprise programme: a strategy', *Irish Business and Administrative Research*, 10,1989, 45-58.

HASLAM, R.B. and COLLINS, N., 'Local government finance in the Republic of Ireland: the aftermath of rates abolition', *Local Government Finance: International Perspectives*, edited by R. Paddison and S. Bailey, London: Croom Helm, 1988, 218-229.

HEDERMAN O'BRIEN, M., 'Whatever happened to rates? A study of Irish tax policy on domestic dwellings', *Administration* 37, 4, 1989, 334-345.

HOGAN, G. and MORGAN, D., *Administrative Law*, London: Sweet and Maxwell Irish Law Texts 1986.

HOURIHAN, K., 'Community policy in Cork: awareness, attitudes and correlates', *Economic and Social Review* 18, 1, October 1986, 17-41.

HOURIHAN, K., 'The impact of urbanisation on municipal government in Ireland', *Administration* 34, 2, 1986, 221-232.

HOURIHAN, K., 'In-migration to Irish cities and towns, 1970-1971', *Economic and Social Review* 14, 1, October 1982, 29-40.

HOURIHAN, K., 'Local community investment and participation in neighbourhood watch: A case study in Cork, Ireland', *Urban Studies* 24, 2, April 1987, 129-136.

INCORPORATED LAW SOCIETY OF IRELAND, *The law directory* (annual) Dublin: 1982-.

INSTITUTE OF PUBLIC ADMINISTRATION, *Administration yearbook and diary* Dublin: IPA 1982-.

INSTITUTE OF PUBLIC ADMINISTRATION, *Managing into the 1990s — the human factor*, Proceedings of the IPA personnel management conference held in Dublin, 4 March 1989 (6 papers), Dublin: IPA 1989.

INSTITUTE OF PUBLIC ADMINISTRATION/ASSOCIATION OF HEALTH BOARDS IN IRELAND, *Community participation in health planning and decision making*, Papers presented at a conference in Killarney, County Kerry, 13-14 May 1988, Dublin: IPA 1988.

INSTITUTE OF PUBLIC ADMINISTRATION/ASSOCIATION OF HEALTH BOARDS IN IRELAND, *The development of care in the community*, Papers presented at a conference held in Blarney, County Cork, 13-15 May 1986, Dublin: IPA 1986 (Bib.).

INSTITUTE OF PUBLIC ADMINISTRATION/COUNTY AND CITY ENGIN-EERS JOINT CONFERENCE, *The future for local authority engineering*, Papers read at the conference held in Kenmare, County Kerry, 1-3 November 1989, Dublin: IPA 1989.

INSTITUTE OF PUBLIC ADMINISTRATION/LOCAL AUTHORITIES MEM-BERS ASSOCIATION, *Financing development — the role of the structural funds*, Proceedings of a conference held in the Glendevlin Hotel, Dundalk on 31 March and 1 April 1989, Dublin: IPA Library Information File.

INSTITUTE OF PUBLIC ADMINISTRATION/LOCAL AUTHORITIES MEMBERS ASSOCIATION, *Financing local government. Is there a better way?* Proceedings of a conference held at the Hotel Kilkenny, Kilkenny 8-9 April 1988 (5 Papers), Dublin: IPA Library Information File.

IEI, *Value for money in infrastructural development, roads, sanitary services and housing*: a seminar held at Jury's Hotel, Dublin 7 June 1984, Dublin: 1984 (Bib.).

IULA, 'The way ahead', a policy statement of IULA (Adopted by the IULA Executive Committee at its meeting in Istanbul, Turkey 5-6 May 1987, *IULA Newsletter* Supplement 8, 9, September 1987, i-viii.

IULA, 'World wide declaration on local self government', (IULA meeting 27th world congress Rio de Janeiro 23/26 September 1985), *Planning and Administration* 14, 1, Spring 1987, 125-127.

JACKSON, P., 'Training schemes: a dilemma for community work in Ireland', *Community Development Journal* 19, 2, April 1984, 82-87.

JENNINGS, R., 'Housing quality and housing choice', *Administration* Special Issue 36, 4, 1988, 7-21.

JENNINGS, R., 'Kerry revisited: can it solve the land problem?', *Irish Journal of Environmental Science* 2, 2, 1983, 32-36.

JENNINGS, R., 'L.A. housing in order', *LAN(IDA)* Autumn 1989, 1-2.

JENNINGS, R. and GRIST, B., 'The problem with building land', *Administration* 31, 3, 1983, 257-283.

JOINT COMMITTEE ON BUILDING LAND, *Report of the Joint Committee...* (Pl 3232) (Chairperson:Robert Molloy) Dublin: SO 1985.

JOINT COMMITTEE ON THE SECONDARY LEGISLATION OF THE EUROPEAN COMMUNITIES, *Community aid for infrastructural development in Ireland*, Seventy sixth report of the joint committee.... Dublin: SO 1982.

JOYCE, L., and DALY, M., *Towards local planning: an evaluation of the pilot COMTEC programme* Dublin: IPA 1987.

KEANE, M.J., 'Accessibility and urban growth rates: evidence for the Irish urban system', *Economic and Social Review* 15, 2, January 1984, 125-139.

KEANE, M.J., 'Using lotteries to pay for roads: a note of caution', *Irish Journal of Environmental Science* 3, 2, 1986, 34-37 (Bib.).

KEANE, R., 'The constitution and public administration: accountability and the public service, administrative law and planning law', *Administration* 35, 4, 1987, 128-142.

KEANE, R., 'Land use, compensation and the community', *Irish Jurist* XVIII, NS 1983, 23-33.

KEANE, R., 'The law of local government in the Republic of Ireland', Dublin: Incorporated Law Society of Ireland 1982.

KEATING, S., *Development plans*. A paper presented to the IDA/LAMA annual conference held in Galway 24/25 April 1987, Dublin: IPA Library Information File.

KEILTHY, J., 'Water rates collection falls flat', *Business and Finance* 26 April 1984, 34.

KELLY, J., 'Urban renewal in Dublin', *L.A.N.(Nestron)* 2, 6, 1989, 13-.

KELLY, P.J., *The role of the councillor as seen through the eyes of a councillor*, Address given at the LAMA conference for newly elected councillors at Two Mile Inn, County Clare 16 November 1985 Dublin: IPA Library Information File.

KELLY, V., 'Focus on clients: A reappraisal of the effectiveness of TDs' interventions', *Administration* 35, 2, 1987, 130-151.

KOMITO, L., 'Voters, politicians and clientelism: a Dublin survey', *Administration* 37, 2, 1989, 171-196.

L.A.N.(Nestron) 'Cork: the developing city', 1, 2, 1987, 3-.

'Designated areas scheme extended', 1, 6, 1988 38-.

'Dublin Corporation — a profile', 1, 1, 1987, 4-.

'Dundalk development plans — designated areas scheme a major boost to towns', 2, 1, 1988 4-.

'Kilkenny city — preservation and urban renewal', 1, 3, 1987, 13-.

'Limerick revitalised — the work of the inner city projects team', 1, 4, 1987, 23-.

'Local authority environment campaign awards', 2, 6, 1989, 8-.

'Urban renewal Wexford', 2, 2, 1988, 3-.

LEECH, B., CABOT, D. and SMYTH, S., *Job creation potential in Ireland arising from community and national environmental legislation* (3 vols), Dublin: Foras Forbartha 1985.

LAMA, *Councillor/manager relations*, Paper presented at the LAMA conference for newly elected councillors at Two Mile Inn, County Clare 16 November 1985, Dublin: IPA Library Information File.

LAN (IPA), 'Cleaning up on water (the Local Government (Water Pollution) (Amendment) Bill 1989)', Autumn 1989, 3.

'Councillors fare well in election', Spring 1987, 4.

'Framework for development (the community support framework)', Winter 1989/90, 1-2.

'Index to parliamentary questions relating to local authorities', Autumn 1987, 8; Spring 1988, 7-8; Autumn 1989, 7-8; Winter 1989/90, 7-8.

'Supreme court ruling against water charges', Spring 1987, 3.

LUCY, J., *Planning in the local authority service — the engineering involvement*, A lecture to the annual conference of the County and City Engineers Association held in Kinsale 29 October 1985, Dublin: IPA Library Information File.

LUKE, G., 'The cost of quality in the inner city [of Dublin]', *Business and Finance* 20 September 1984, 31.

LUKE, G., 'Council cash crisis — the options', *Business and Finance* 6 October 1983, 9-10.

LUKE, G., 'Land tax and lotteries: two cash raising options for L.A.s', *Business and Finance* 6 October 1983, 11-12.

LYNCH, M., 'Environmental impacts of planning legislation', *The Environmentalist* II, 1 Autumn 1988, 4-5.

MacGREIL, M., 'Housing: a community service and a social responsibility', *Social Studies* 9, 3-4 Spring 1987, 29-38..

MANSERGH, N., 'The taxation of development land', *Administration* 30, 4, 1982, 114-128.

MAWHINNEY, K., 'Local authorities and historical and architectural conservation', *Irish Journal of Environmental Science* 4, 1, 1986, 29-34 (Bib.).

McCARRON, E.G., 'Planning for living (in the Dublin area)', *The Engineers Journal* 37, 10 October 1983, 25-28.

McCOLGAN, J., *British policy and the Irish administration 1920-22*, London: Allen and Unwin, 1983.

McDONALD, F., *Local government: does it exist in Ireland?* (a 2 part series of articles) 'Where the mandarins of Merrion St. rule,' page 7; 'Councils powerless as power is whittled away,' page 11, *Irish Times* 26 and 27 April 1990.

McGEE, J., 'Councils — domestic charges trickle in', *Business and Finance* 8 December 1988, 34-35.

McDOWELL, M., *Financing local authorities: the questionable viability of a local property tax*, Dublin: UCD Centre for Economic Research Policy Paper 2, 1988, 23 (Bib.).

McGEE, J. and O'KEEFFE, S., 'The cash dries up for the councils', *Business and Finance* 7 April 1988, 14-16.

McGEE, J. and O'KEEFFE, S., 'Clare cottons on to the lottery game', *Business and Finance* 7 April 1988, 15, 17-19.

McKAY, P., 'Last chance for Cork [for the car ferry link between Cork and Wales]', *Business and Finance* 14 May 1987, 30-31.

McNAMARA, T., 'Local government is a minority interest', *Irish Times* 4 January 1989, 7.

McNAMARA, T., *Local government — the future*, Summary of address to locally elected representatives' seminar, Kilkenny, 9 November 1985 Dublin: IPA Library Information File.

McNAMARA, T., *Local government reform — devolution of power*, Paper prepared for the County and City Engineers Conference, Killarney 8 November 1984 Dublin: IPA Library Information File.

MEEHAN, B., *Planning in local authorities: a time for review*, Paper presented to the IDA/LAMA annual conference held in Galway 24-25 April 1987 Dublin: IPA Library Information File.

MOLONEY, M., 'Cork — up-grading and modernising its housing stock', *L.A.N. (Nestron)* 4, 4, 1990, 19-.

MORAN, S., 'Limerick — long standing problems being tackled', *L.A.N.(Nestron)* 3, 2, 1989, 25-.

MOXON-BROWNE, E. and MUNDAY, J., 'Bridges and chasms: cross cutting attitudes among district councillors in Northern Ireland', *Administration* 32, 1, 1984, 55-75.

MUINTIR NA TÍRE, *Towards a new democracy: implications of local government reform* Dublin: IPA, 1985 (Bib.).

MULREANY, M., 'Facing up to the cuts: the main aspects of the 1987 budget and the implications for local authority planning', *LAN (IPA)* Spring 1987, 1-3.

MURPHY, D., *Local government superannuation in practice: model procedure charts for granting benefits to pensionable officers, pensionable servants, registered officers, registered employees.* (2nd ed.) Dublin: IPA 1986 (Looseleaf in 5 sections).

MURPHY, T.G., '"Kowloon Bridge" the local authority experience', *L.A.N.(Nestron)* 1, 2, 1987, 21-.

NATIONAL PLANNING BOARD, *Proposals for plans 1984-1987* Dublin: SO 1984.

NURRE, D., *Contracting out of local services: analysis of an option for local authorities: the case of refuse collection* Dublin: IPA 1987.

O'CARROLL, J.P., 'Community programmes and the traditional view of community', *Social Studies* 8, 3/4 Spring/Summer 1985, 138-148.

O'CARROLL, J.P., 'Strokes, cute hoors and sneaking regarders: the influence of local culture on Irish political style', *Irish Political Studies* 2, 1987, 77-92.

Ó CEALLAIGH, M.B., 'Computing in Irish local government', *L.A.N.(Nestron)* 1, 1, 1987, 15-.

Ó CEARBHAILL, D. and Ó CINNÉIDE, M.S., 'Community development in the west of Ireland: a case study of the Killala area', *Community Development Journal* 21, 3 July 1986, 195-206 (Bib.).

Ó CINNÉIDE, S., 'Community response to unemployment', *Administration* 33, 2, 1985, 231-257.

O'CONNOR, D. 'Water supply optimisation by district metering', *L.A.N. (Nestron)* 2, 3, 1988, 17-.

O'CONNOR, J. and DALY, M., *Transition and change in the mid west of Ireland: a base line study of west Limerick* (2 vols), Limerick: NIHE Social Research Centre 1983 (Bib.).

O'CONNOR, M., 'Cork — rehabilitating low-cost housing', *L.A.N.(Nestron)* 3, 2, 1989, 13-.

O'CONNOR, S., *Community care services: an overview,* Dublin: NESC Report 84 (Pl 4972) October 1987.

O'DONOGHUE, M., 'Response to Miriam Hederman O'Brien's "A study of Irish tax policy on domestic dwellings"', *Administration* 37, 4, 1989, 346-351.

O'DONOHUE, F., 'The situation in Ireland', *Poverty in Europe* — IULA's attempts to gather experiences of local authorities in Europe. IULA seminar, Brussels 8-9 December 1983, *IULA Newsletter* April 1984, 4-5.

O'DONOVAN, F., 'Cork's sale of the century (local authority tenant purchase scheme)', *Business and Finance* 13 April 1989, 18.

O'FLYNN, J.S., 'Trade effluent charges — is the polluter really paying?', *L.A.N.(Nestron)* 2, 5, 1988, 21-.

O'GORMAN, N.T. and O'CARROLL, T.A., 'The dilemma of Irish economic development: perspectives on the evolution of Ireland's public finances and economy from the early 1960s to the mid 1980s', *Journal of the Statistical and Social Inquiry Society of Ireland* XXV, IV, 1986/1987, 127-177.

O'HAGAN, J., McBRIDE, P. and SANFEY, P., 'Local government finance: the Irish experience', *British Tax Review* 4, 1985, 235-254.

O'HAGAN, J., McBRIDE, P. and SANFEY, P., 'Local revenue sources for local government: the continuing debate', *Administration* 34, 2, 1986, 233-253.

O'KEEFFE, S., 'The £5000 grants run into snags', *Business and Finance* 4 July 1985, 29-31.

O'NEILL, F., 'Limerick — urban regeneration and the designated area', *L.A.N.(Nestron)* 3, 3, 1989, 3-.

O'REGAN, J., ' Funding and the current state of Irish roads', *The Engineers Journal* 37, 8 August 1983, 47-48.

OSBORNE, M., 'Those county managers' *The Bell* 9, 4, January 1945, 304-12.

O'SULLIVAN, G., 'Local authorities and the new safety legislation', *L.A.N.(Nestron)* 4, 4, 1990, 15-.

O'SULLIVAN, J., 'Cargo of uncertainty ("Kowloon Bridge"): a summary of the seminar organised by UCD Environmental Policy Centre and the Maritime Institute of Ireland', *LAN (IPA)* Spring 1987, 6.

O'SULLIVAN, J., 'EIA: planning a better environment (a guide for local authorities)', *LAN (IPA)* Winter 1989/90, 4-7.

O'SULLIVAN, P. and SHEPHERD, K., *A source book on planning law in Ireland,* Abingdon, Oxford: Professional Books Ltd. 1984, XXXVIII + 568, Supplement 1987, 217.

O'TOOLE, A., 'The big housing sell off. Are the local authorities and the exchequer losing out?', *Business and Finance* 3 February 1983, 15.

PARKER, A.J., 'The "friends and neighbours" voting effect in the Galway West constituency, 1977', *Political Geography Quarterly* 1/3, 1982, 243-262.

PARKER, A.J., 'Localism and bailiwicks: The Galway West Constituency in the 1977 general election', *Proceedings Royal Irish Academy* 83c/2, 1983, 17-36.

PHILIPPOVICH, T., *Organising for a stronger voice: the role of local authority associations.* Paper presented at a seminar organised by the Irish Council for the European Movement on 'The crisis in local government', and held in Dublin on 12/13 October 1982, Dublin: Irish Council for the European Movement 1982.

POWER, C., '1992 — a new lease of life for local authorities', *L.A.N.(Nestron)* 2, 6, 1989, 3-.

PUBLIC LIBRARY SERVICE REVIEW GROUP, report of the public library service review group, Dublin, Stationery Office, 1987.

RICE, T.P., 'The revenue finances of local authorities', *Administration* 30, 1, 1982, 16-32.

RIGAL, J., 'Some issues concerning the integration of Irish travellers', *Administration* 37, 1, 1989, 87-93.

ROCHE, D., 'Local government', *Administration* 30, 2/3, 1982, 133-146.

ROCHE, D., *Local government in Ireland,* Dublin: IPA 1982 (Bib.).

RONAYNE, L., 'The public library authority: a time for reforms', *Irish Library* SS 4, 4, 1987, 99-109.

ROSEINGRAVE, J., 'EC funds: letting the regions decide', *Irish Times* 6 January 1985, 9.

RIA, and DOE, *Housing in the eighties*: proceedings of the 1981 national housing conference, Dublin: Foras Forbartha, 1982 (Bib.).

RYAN, E., 'Who gets the big housing contracts: local authority building in Dublin', *Business and Finance* 5 May 1983, 22.

RYAN, F. and McNAMARA, J., *Local authorities in action: a training package and educational source book* (2 vols) Dublin: IPA 1983 (Looseleaf).

RYAN, T., 'Time to re-assess the role of local government: who's calling the tune?', *Irish Times* 4 April 1990, 16.

SCANNELL, Y., *The law and practice relating to pollution control in Ireland* (2nd ed.) London: Graham & Trotman Ltd for CEC 1982.

SCANNELL, Y., 'Planning control: twenty years on (Part 1)', *Dublin University Law Journal* NS 4, 1982, 41-67.

SCANNELL, Y., 'Planning control: twenty years on (Part II)', *Dublin University Law Journal* NS 5, December 1983, 225-247.

SHAFFREY, P., *Building of Irish towns*, Dublin: O'Brien Press, 1983.

SHAFFREY, P. (ed.), *Your guide to planning*, Dublin: O'Brien Press and An Taisce in association with the Irish Planning Institute, 1983.

SHERIDAN, J., 'Dublin corporation's insurance — a new policy', *L.A.N.(Nestron)* 2, 2, 1988, 32-.

SO, *The way forward*, National economic plan 1983-1987 Dublin: 1983.

SO, *Local elections 1985*, Election results and transfer of votes in respect of each county and county borough council and election statistics relating to all local authorities (Pl 3578) Dublin: 1986.

SO, *Building on reality 1985-1987* Dublin: 1984.

STEVENSON, C.P., 'Negotiated planning: circumventing the planning system: I + II', *Irish Jurist* NS XIX, 1984, 15-39, 226-248.

STEWART, J.J., 'Investment in infrastructure — the need and the reality', *The Engineers Journal* 38, 5, May 1985, 41-44.

STOKER, E.B., 'Cork corporation, new town development at Mahon Peninsula', *The Engineers Journal* 37, 8 August 1983, 49-51.

STOUT, R., *Administrative Law in Ireland* Dublin: IPA 1985.

SULLIVAN, M., 'Dublin city: environment and accessibility: a traffic engineer's view', *The Engineers Journal* 40, 4, April 1987, 14-18.

SWEENEY, N., 'Waste collection and disposal in Co. Offaly', *L.A.N.(Nestron)* 1, 3, 1987, 37-.

TAAFFE, J., *The role and function of the councillor*, Paper given at the conference for elected representatives, Mullingar 12 October 1985 Dublin: IPA Library Information File.

TOVEY, M., '"Local community": in defence of a much criticised concept', *Social Studies* 8, 3/4 Spring/Summer 1985, 149-163.

TRAVELLING PEOPLE REVIEW BODY, *Report of the travelling people review body* (Chairperson:Walter MacEvilly) (Pl 1552) Dublin: SO February 1983.

VAN DER KAMP, H., *Planning statistics 1985*, Dublin: Foras Forbartha, 1986.

VAN DER KAMP, H., *Regional planning: a review of regional studies* Dublin:Foras Forbartha, 1987 (Bib.).

WALKER, G.A., 'European Year of the Environment and the local authorities', *L.A.N.(Nestron)* 1, 1, 1987, 31-.

WALSH, A., 'The role of the local authority [in housing policy]', *Administration* Special Issue 36, 4, 1988, 52-58.

WARD, G., 'Charging users — lessons from local authority experience', *Promise and performance: Irish environmental policies analysed*, edited by J. Blackwell and F. Convery, Dublin: UCD Resource and Environmental Policy Centre 1983, 377-382.

WARD, J.G., 'Securing income to pay for local authority services', *L.A.N.(Nestron)* 2, 4, 1988, 3-.

WEAFER, J., 'Urban community: dead or alive', *Social Studies* 8, 3/4 Spring/Summer 1985, 179-187.

WHITE, P., 'Some issues the city must face [Dublin]', *Business and Finance* Special Supplement June 1983, 13, 15.

WORKING GROUP ON COST OVER RUNS ON PUBLIC CONSTRUCTION CONTRACTS, *Report of the working group...* (Chairperson:A. Kearns) Dublin: SO 1983.

YOUTH EMPLOYMENT AGENCY, *Development of community enterprise in Ireland*: a report on the community enterprise consultative forum jointly organised by the YEA and the European Community Development Exchange in January 1987, Dublin: YEA 1987.

ZIMMERMAN, T.F., 'Regional governance models: greater Dublin and greater London', *National Civic Review* 71, 2, February 1982, 84-90.

APPENDIX 1
COUNTY AND CITY
MANAGERS' ASSOCIATION
Chairmen 1943-1990

The County Management Act 1940 came into operation on 26 August 1942. At an inaugural meeting held at the Gresham Hotel, Dublin on 20 January 1943, the County Managers formed the County Managers' Association and invited the City Managers to join with them. On the acceptance of that invitation by the City Managers, the name of the Association was changed to the County and City Managers' Association at the second meeting on 21 October, 1943. The chairmen of the Association and their terms of office are as follows:

1943-47	William F. Quinlan
1947-53	Philip Monahan
1953-54	Patrick J. Meghen
1954-55	Liam Raftis
1955-56	Sean D. MacLochlainn
1956-57	Clement I. O'Flynn
1957-60	Michael A. Veale
1960-63	John P. Flynn
1963-64	Tomas F. Broe
1964-66	Matthew Macken
1966-69	James L. MacKell
1969-72	Denis M. Candy
1972-75	Joseph Boland
1975-76	Tomás P. MacDiarmada
1976-77	Desmond Williams
1977-78	Michael N. Conlon
1978-79	Patrick Dowd
1979-80	Richard B. Haslam
1980-82	Seamus Keating
1982-84	Francis J. O'Brien
1984-86	John F. Cassidy
1986-88	Michael J. Boyce
1988-90	John G. Ward

APPENDIX 2
ADDRESS BY
SEAN LEMASS, TD
MINISTER FOR SUPPLIES
ON THE APPOINTMENT
OF EMERGENCY
COMMISSIONERS

Radio Éireann, 19 July 1940

In the course of the broadcast, Mr Lemass said: 'The Government itself may be put out of action or cut off from communication with the country by hostilities in the vicinity of the capital. It is necessary, therefore, to set up now an organisation which will ensure that, in any such eventuality, the business of the Government will nevertheless be carried on — that is to say, the preservation of order, the maintenance of essential services such as the public health services, the continuance of unemployment assistance payments, old age pensions and similar forms of public health to the needy; the control of supplies and the like.

The Government has taken steps to that end. It is necessary that the public should know what those steps are, so that they will be able to co-operate fully in making them effective. It should of course be clearly understood that machinery, established to deal with such an emergency as is contemplated, will not begin to function, except for the purpose of preparation, until the emergency has, in fact, arisen, by which I mean, unless by reason of active hostilities proceeding on our territory, some part of the country is wholly cut off from the rest of it, or from contact with the Central Government, and the Government is prevented by such conditions from carrying out its proper functions in that part.

What we are doing, in preparation for such a situation, is to appoint in a number of selected regions and in every county, officers who will act for the Government in the administration of these public services and who will be fully authorised, empowered and instructed to take over control of the existing administrative machinery in their areas and to direct it on their own initiative until contact with the Central Government has been restored. The officers who have been chosen for this work are all experienced men who are now holding responsible positions in the public service. The Regional Commissioners, as we may call them, are civil servants chosen from various departments on grounds of personal suitability and because they can be released immediately to organise this machine. The County Commissioners are officials resident in each county and familiar with its problems. The names of these officers will be published shortly together with particulars of the regions for which they will be responsible.

The County Commissioners will act under the direction and control of the Regional Commissioners, who will delegate such powers and functions as are necessary. In the event of hostilities making it impossible to maintain regional organisation or preventing the Regional

Commissioner maintaining contact with any county, the County Commissioners will assume complete responsibility.

Wide Powers

The functions which these Commissioners will discharge in their areas include:

(1) The preservation and conservation of supplies of foodstuffs and fuel; the restriction of consumption and regulation of distribution in case of shortage.

(2) The maintenance of essential public health services, such as water supply, cleansing services, and the prevention of disease and epidemics.

(3) The maintenance of order with the co-operation of the Civic Guard.

(4) Relief of distress of all kinds.

(5) The maintenance of payments in respect of old age pensions, unemployment pay, widows' pensions, soldiers' dependants' allowances, and the like.

It should, of course, be understood that in areas where active military operations are proceeding, the military authorities will be in complete control and in these areas those civil officers will carry out their functions subject to the directions of the military authorities.

It is necessary also to face the fact that portions of our territory may for a time be occupied by an enemy, but even in such case these civil administrators will endeavour to carry on their duties and to provide generally for the welfare of the people until other arrangements are made.

Behind the County Commissioners will be the voluntary parish committee which the Department of Local Government are now arranging to have set up in all areas. These parish committees will have useful and necessary functions to perform even if actual invasion does not occur; functions on behalf of the Department of Supplies, the ARP authorities and other Government Departments; but it is clear that they can be of very useful assistance to the County Commissioners if and when those Commissioners are called upon to undertake their responsibilities. I trust, therefore, that efforts will be made forthwith to establish them everywhere. The completion of our preparations against any or all emergencies cannot be delayed, and the establishment of these committees is an important part of them. In the last resort they can provide the elements of government in their districts should they become

187

isolated until such time as the Central Government is able to restore its authority.

A very great deal of organisational work is necessary to make the plan complete; financial arrangements to enable the commissioners to provide funds and currency to meet local needs; administrative arrangements to ensure the transfer to the regional authorities of control of sections of the nation-wide unemployment assistance service and other social services; arrangements in relation to postal services, lighting services, and the like. These things are being tackled as rapidly as is possible.

Prepare for the Worst

The emergency against which these arrangements are being made may never arise. We trust it never will. But we cannot allow our hopes to guide our counsels. While hoping for the best, we must prepare for the worst and prepare quickly. But if the emergency does arise, I ask everybody to realise that his personal safety and the welfare of all our people will depend entirely on the fullness of the public co-operation with the Government plans. The Emergency Commissioners will have colossal tasks to face and will require the maximum of help from all good citizens. Their decrees must be loyally obeyed. They will act with the authority of the National Government, and disobedience to their orders will be disloyalty to the nation. They will be the last bulwark against anarchy, and on the effective discharge of their duties the health and, perhaps, the very lives, of great numbers of our people will depend. All citizens must, voluntarily and willingly, stand behind them.

Stay Put

All arrangements made in advance, no matter how carefully planned, will break down if people stampede in large numbers from one district to another. Food distribution, protection against violence, the maintenance of health services, even the provision of shelter, may become impossible unless people stay where they are until orders to leave have been given by the military authorities. Our advice to you, therefore, should an attack be made on this country, is to stay where you are at the time, until active hostilities have stopped or the military authorities order you to move. Stay where you are and obey the instructions of the local officers of the Government. By doing so you will minimise the risk to yourself and make it easier for the Government to reduce the consequences of such attack on our people as a whole.'